The Big Conservation Lie

The Untold Story of Wildlife Conservation in Kenya

John Mbaria & Mordecai Ogada
2016

DEDICATION

To our Ancestors, who lived with, used, and conserved our biodiversity without being paid crumbs to do so.
To those of us who struggle today to wrest this most precious resource from the grip of an avaricious elite.
And to our children and the unborn who, we hope, will appreciate this bounty and never forget that it is their birthright.

CONTENTS

ACKNOWLEDGMENTS

This book has been a very long time in the making, not because of the time taken to write it, but the combined years of experience in different fields that yielded this collection of thoughts. We would like to sincerely thank all those who crossed our paths and nourished us intellectually. We would like to mention the following, Dorothy Wanja Nyingi, Joyce Nyairo, Michela Wrong, Wanjiku Kiambo, Andy Hill, Laurence Frank, the late Anthony King, and William Pike.

There are others who took us through life's lessons, whipped us into line, and enabled us to eventually realize this and other dreams. With fond memories, we mention Francis Mbaria, Mary Waithera, the late Evans Kamau (a former English teacher of Kibubuti Primary School), Mwalimu Bulderick Ogange, Purity Kendi, and Ali Nadim Zaidi. We specially thank Ambassador Nehamiah Rotich for ably demonstrating that local talent and professionalism is what is needed to effectively manage the Kenya Wildlife Service.

This book has been a journey in discovery of our country, our society, our traditions, our weaknesses, and our strengths. In the discussions we had on social media, there were so many friends who shared insights, thoughts, and encouragement that made us see the value of this work, long before it was complete. David T. Mbogori, Loiuza Kabiru, Said Wabera, Koikai Oliotiptip, Mali Ole Kaunga, Dennis Morton, Kiama Kaara, Alexia Trombas, Franky Kago, Noni Mbatia, Gichena Chacha, Salisha Chandra, Kipruto Kertiony, Kariuki Kiragu, Pieter Kat, Hawi Odingo, Mutemi wa Kiama, Njenga Kahiiu, Elizabeth Wamba, Mike Mills, Nelson ole Reiyia, Leonard Lenina Mpoke, Leonard Omullo, Munene Kilongi, and Geoffrey Kamadi

Last but not least, Skeeter Wilson, for believing in our work, and Trevor O'Hara, John Nyagah, and Eddie Obinju for your respective roles in making this a reality.

Our sincere gratitude to you all.

The Epiphany

John Mbaria's Encounter With Unseen Injustice

She was an unmistakable image of deprivation. The emaciated Samburu woman had thrown across her left shoulder a torn *shuka*, which left parts of her body exposed. She had braved the sweltering Samburu sun that baked the entire place bringing into being mirages of promise that failed to deliver more than that. As she advanced to the river, the woman attempted an upright position. But her stooped frame refused to yield. Nevertheless, this enabled me to peer into her cracked, multilined face. Her look was distant. Her thin hands held onto a cord with which she had strapped the empty twenty-litre water jerrican. Her entire frame talked of many struggles and probably as many defeats. The woman had emerged from a thick bush across the river, itself part of a natural spread dotted here and there by short, sturdy trees and broken, now and then, by awkward-looking hills. Some of the outcrops had been whitened by excrement from birds of prey. The vast, monotonous terrain extended into the distant horizon, giving packs, herds and flocks, and other residents a veritable abode. Some did not just live and let live; they visited local people's homesteads with danger and intent. Across the river was a scene removed from the reality of this unforgiving landscape. Under the watchful eyes of armed rangers, a group of us were happily and noisily climbing a rocky landform that formed part of the river's embankment.

This was in 2001, and most of us were young, joyful journalists. We had been sponsored to the Shaba Game Reserve, 314 kilometres northeast of Nairobi, by the Sarova Group of Hotels, one of Kenya's most prominent hotel chains with eight hotels—many of which are carefully stashed in some of Kenya's most spectacular, most pristine pieces of wilderness. Located in Eastern Kenya, Shaba is where the popular reality TV adventure series *Survivor III* was shot in August 2001. Before that, the game reserve hosted Joy and George Adamson, the romantic conservationists who gave the world a reality show of life in the bush before they were tragically murdered. Together with its sister reserve, Buffalo Springs, Shaba boasts of seventeen springs that sojourn along subterranean courses from Mount Kenya—one

1

hundred or so kilometres away—and which gush out there to convert part of this dry wasteland into a veritable oasis. Along its northern boundary flows the Ewaso Nyiro River that, together with the springs, has made the entire place a magnet for gerenuks, Grevy's zebras, reticulated giraffes, lions, leopards, and hundreds of bird species that live side by side with the Samburu people. We were taken there to savour the unmitigated joy of spending time in a purely wild area. We were expected to reciprocate by meeting our brief—flowery feature stories embellished into captivating narratives that could attract and keep guests visiting the hotel and the reserve. Many of us were poorly paid cub reporters who could hardly afford the European cuisine on offer or the joys of partaking of a game drive atop four-wheel-drive fuel guzzlers. With a monthly pay that either equaled or was slightly more than the cost of spending a night in the extremely comfortable and luxurious hotel, we could not but agree to be spoiled for three days and be blinded by freebies. We roamed the area in vans packed with bites, booze, and soda. For lunch and dinner, three-course meals of continental dishes awaited—a veritable feeding frenzy ensued.

While on game drives, we hoped to spot elephants, dung beetles, and everything in between. Part of our exclusive experience included climbing a rocky landform close to the crocodile-infested Ewaso Nyiro River. It was while doing so that I spotted the elderly Samburu woman. Silently—almost in mime—and removed from my world, she was to take me through a host of lessons that dramatically altered my entire outlook on the grand wildlife conservation program Kenya and other countries in Africa have adopted since the dawn of colonialism.

For some reason, I found myself thoughtfully watching her every move. She dipped her jerrican into the river, rapidly filling it with the muddy, unpalatable water. The water notwithstanding, this had me thinking. With a load of European food still fresh in my belly, I could afford to summon some imagination. I conjured images of the immense peril the woman had exposed herself to. But what repeatedly danced in my mind was one image in which a four-metre, several-hundred-kilo crocodile emerged from the water, splashed dirty water into her eyes, and in a lightning move, grabbed the woman's leg with its massive jaws, its saw-like teeth tearing into her flesh, as it then dragged her limp body into the deeper waters. In my mind's eye, the croc went on to convert her entire existence into some unsightly bloody mess.

Thank God this did not happen. But in the case it had happened, I figured that it would have resulted in several eventualities: A photojournalist would have captured the bloody scene in a single, award-winning shot. The woman would have paid the ultimate price, ending up as yet another sad statistic. Many of us would have filed copious media reports detailing how "another victim met her death" or "I witnessed the worst case of human-wildlife conflict at the banks of Ewaso." KWS rangers would have been summoned. And with cocked guns, fingers on triggers, eyes strained to the river, and adrenaline pumping into muscles, they would have first shot in the air to rattle any crocs. The rangers would have found it impossible to identify the culprit. Unable to isolate the life-snatching beast from the rest of the gang, they would have shot one of them—an act of appeasement to sorrowful relatives, tit-for-tat killing, justice delivered to a woman so shunned in life. The conservation juggernaut would have rolled on, as ever deceitful and callously removed from the plight of those who suffer the brunt of what it purports to preserve.

Yes, the woman lived that day, not just to take the dirty water home, but probably to go back to the river and risk her life many more times. Maybe she lived only to fall sick or die from the muddy, parasite-infested Ewaso waters. This is not just a possibility. Neither is it a mere probability or likelihood. It is a circumstance that is replicated countless times across most areas bordering Kenya's twenty-two national parks and twenty-eight national reserves. Many of the people who live with wildlife in Africa meet their deaths, leaving hordes of orphans with no one to wipe their tears. There are hundreds of women—young and old — who have been denied the comfort of travelling through life with their spouses. There are men who must gnash their teeth in pain and immense anger each time they think of their late beloved spouses and children. There are countless more who live without limbs, just as there are many others who endure torn flesh, broken bones, blindness, destitution, and loss of entire livelihoods occasioned by encounters with wild animals.

In this Samburu woman, I saw the embodiment of a community praised for its traditional conservation ethics that spared for the world vast populations of diverse wildlife, a community, however, shunned by the world, even as acres of paper and decades of airtime are expended by many a conservationist and organization to discuss their welfare.

Upon this revelation, I refused to play along, and I made it my career to expose the rot.

~ John Mbaria, 2014

Mordecai Ogada's Rude Awakening.

Kilimanjaro stood majestically over the Amboseli plains, timeless, distant, yet as imposing as ever. I sat in the dining area at Tortilis Camp, thinking over and over again at how perfect this setting and how well-chosen the spot. My thoughts were also revolving around Embarinkoi Hill, a nondescript, thirty-metre high mound of volcanic rock and soil. It was 2008, and I was on assignment as the manager of the Kenya Wildlife Trust, a job with which I was quite satisfied, not least because my office was nestled in the leafy, pleasant surroundings of Karen, one of the more affluent suburbs of Nairobi. The Kenya Wildlife Trust was then a new NGO, formed as a partnership between a number of luxury camping safari firms led by Ker & Downey Safaris. Ker & Downey Safaris was established in 1946 and moved from being a hunting safari operator to operating luxury camping and photographic tours. Their guest list over the years is a stunning roster of the Western world's rich and famous from the spheres of politics, business, and the arts. A typical K&D camping safari begins with the guide visiting the client at home in the United States or Europe several months in advance. During this visit, the safari is custom-designed, from the arrival date and itinerary down to the smallest detail, such as gourmet menus and what wines will be served with what food out in the wilderness. It is a service worthy of the $1,100 to $1,200 per person per day charged by the operators to their well-heeled guests.

These camping activities are carried out in Kitirua, a 30,000-acre wildlife habitat that is an extension of the Amboseli National Park ecosystem. For the use of this particular wildlife habitat, there is an agreement between K&D and the Olgulului-Ololarashi Group ranches by which they pay lease fees and implement other corporate social responsibility initiatives. These initiatives are

4

primarily designed to demonstrate to the local community that conservation is worth their trouble. The Kenya Wildlife Trust was set up as a structure to manage and implement these initiatives, and I was the brand new trust manager, eager to make a difference in this community. By that point, there was only one thing that I found troubling about my new job. I had earlier been invited to our board chairman's magnificent residence in Karen, and he shared his vision for Kitirua over drinks. We were shielded from the evening chill and unwanted (if friendly) interruptions from his pedigree ridgeback dogs by the huge bay windows overlooking the swimming pool. An examination of my surroundings and rudimentary calculations led me to realize that the annual lease fee paid by K&D to be shared by the entire Olgulului community for the exclusive use of Kitirua was less than what it would cost to rent this house for a similar period. This was a wonderful residence set in a beautiful, mature garden with a magnificent view of the Ngong Hills. However, Kitirua was 30,000 acres of prime wildlife habitat with a magnificent view of Kilimanjaro, not to mention elephants, cheetahs, lions, and numerous other species of charismatic wildlife. Most importantly, it was also the birthright of several thousand Maasai. This arrangement was at best exploitative, and in my mind, its only saving grace was its impending expiry and likely review.

My reverie was interrupted by the Tortilis Camp manager asking whether I would like a drink. Since he was a partner in this project, I decided to ask why on Earth the wonderful school and market we were building was located way behind Embarinkoi Hill. To be honest, I was mildly irritated that I had been required to drive so far in the dust. I was taken aback when he flippantly told me that it was necessary to move the Maasai community behind the hill so that their *manyattas* wouldn't sully tourists' view of Kilimanjaro.

That hot afternoon in Amboseli, I experienced my road to Damascus. I realized that I was part of a system that had no respect for the very bedrock on which it stood. I was a qualified black face put in place to smooth over fifty years of exploitation in two and to create a pleasant backdrop that would allow for the renewal of this insidious arrangement. The technical knowledge I had from all the years and energy I spent studying conservation biology weren't important here. The Dr. prefix to my name, my knowledge of Kiswahili, and my complexion were all props to make things appear honest. These realizations came to me in a merciless flood, and I was momentarily filled with outrage and self-loathing. I was part of a fallacy whose sell-by date was fast approaching.

My immediate reaction was to start searching for another job. Whether my self-respect was restored by my next job is in part the story of this book, which I knew someday, somehow I had to tell. This book is for those of us involved in conservation and give of ourselves towards this noble principle, and if it makes us take another look in the mirror and makes others think more carefully about us, then mission accomplished.

~ Mordecai O. Ogada, 2014

1 ~ How Did We Get Here?

The importance of imagery: Kenya used over 10,000 litres of diesel and kerosene to burn over one hundred tons of ivory in an exercise whose benefit remains to be seen, other than in the dramatic images it produced. (©Raabia Hawa)

Have you ever seen a black man aired on Animal Planet?," asked a Nigerian comedian, Bright Okpocha, better known by his stage name, Basketmouth. Okopcha asked this during an Aljazeera TV Program on February 16, 2016. The audience became silent. Then the immensely popular stand-up comedian volunteered to explain the courage with which white people aired on the television channel usually advance on some dangerous animal. "White people are never afraid. They only become afraid when you go to the embassy seeking a visa . . . They tell you, 'I am afraid we cannot give you a visa.'" Said in an officious mimic, this drew instant laughter from the audience.

Though said in jest, Okpocha's observation is indicative of how we got where we are as far as wildlife conservation in many African countries is concerned. Animal Planet is an American cable television channel owned by Discovery Communications that immerses viewers in scintillating reality stunts exclusively performed by white people before an audience of over ninety-eight million Americans and hundreds of millions from more than seventy other countries. Okopcha might have been joking, but the image of white men (they are mostly male characters) taking to the wild, devoting their lives to saving wild animals, and engaging in sensually captivating adventures has forever been used to drive the point home that as the planet experiences immense destruction of species, habitats, and ecosystems, it is only white people who really care. Conservation is now almost exclusively associated with whiteness.

Most of the characters aired on programs such as on Animal Planet are not even nationals of the relevant countries. They are usually foreigners who are glorified for giving up trademark comforts and jobs and for making contributions to the lives of wild animals. Almost always, the themes in most of the programs revolve around a human character, whose compassion and love for animals is driven by altruism, while his love for adventure is usually not covered. Instead, what is given prominence is how much these characters are involved in doing all that is within their means to protect the lives of some exotic animal species. This theme is repeatedly captured not just on television but also in the largest portion of books, magazines, and feature films on wildlife conservation. The plots are usually thin and straightforward. Usually it is about the pains white adventurers and conservationists go through as they attempt to secure the future of a spectacularly endangered species or an individual animal. Usually, black people are featured either as cargo men, props, victims, or as hindrances to the conservation enterprise. In most instances, black Africans are portrayed as people who need to be sensitized, so that they can either accept or learn to love the animals that live in their midst or the wildernesses they inhabit.

This has gone on despite the fact that many of these black Africans interact with endangered animals on a day-to-day basis. In many cases too, this sensitization is done as an afterthought; it rarely occupies the mainstay of the narrative. Many times, it is done through educational programs that are spiced with different forms of bribery (boreholes, classrooms, school bursaries, dispensaries, and others). But the narrative is passed on in such a manner that what will linger in the mind of the viewer or reader is the image of a truly altruistic white person who perseveres in a situation as he works among animals. This has now assumed a life of its own—it is now associated with the entire wildlife conservation enterprise. These selfless characters have become intertwined with the survival and well-being of individual animal species, if not entire habitats and ecosystems. Later in life, those involved take self-praise to a higher crescendo when they author memoirs that are rarely evaluated against the inconsistencies between before-and-after scenarios.

As we shall see in subsequent chapters, this narrative has left an indelible mark on the subconscious of the people it is intended to influence. Consequently, most Kenyans today exclusively associate wildlife conservation care, compassion, and even ownership with white people. At a time when Africa has more cell phones than Europe, this same old narrative has weathered the storms of modernity. Africans of European descent have continued to advance the same narrative more than one hundred years since Africa's colonialist-driven modernization began. This has more to do with control than anything else.

In *Curing Their Ills: Colonial Power and African Illness*, Megan Vaughan refers to works on colonial ecological history and the imperial hunting cult to explain how European male colonialists perceived and constructed modern Africa and the continent's environment and how this points to a European obsession with control:

> In the late nineteenth and early twentieth century, East and Central Africa Europeans still perceived of themselves as grappling with a wild and uncontrolled environment, of which Africans were an integral part. In part, this was an outcome of

the extension of the separation of 'nature and 'culture' described
. . . as characterizing the development of the nineteenth century
European thought. The 'wild' whether in the form of the
moorland, 'woman,' or African wildlife was simultaneously
romanticized and feared in European culture of the late
nineteenth century. Recent work on colonial ecological history
and on the imperial hunting cult has emphasised the process by
which European male colonialists perceived and constructed
'Africa' and the African environment through this peculiar
cultural lens, and has pointed to the European obsession with
control . . .

Hero Worship

Hero worship in conservation is as old as wildlife conservation
itself. The subjects of this worship are invariably white men and
women who are lionized for taking to a life of selfless service of
the wilderness and its residents. Though they serve in
environments where native Africans have lived for centuries and
have done little more than simply live among animals, they have
continued to receive near-universal adulation. To ensure that the
world does not take a second look at what it deems to be their
heroism and altruism, their misdeeds, failures, and true
personalities are conveniently ignored so to craft as attractive a
narrative as possible.

George Alexander Graham Adamson (George Adamson), the
man who lived with lions in Meru and Kora National Parks, is a
product of this creative storytelling. To those who might not know
much more about him than is said in most reports, books, and
films, the man is nothing short of a conservation saint. Before he
was murdered on August 20, 1989, by bandits, his life in the wilds
of Meru and Kora was, and still is, painted in such glowing terms
that one would be forgiven to feel that those who cast skepticism
on his work and character must be blaspheming. Born in 1906 in
India, Adamson's work is eternalized in movies such as *Born Free*,
its sequel *Living Free*, and *To Walk with Lions*, as well as TV series

and books such as *Lord of the Lions*. Adamson contributed to the
creation of his own myth by writing immensely touching accounts
of his life with lions and his eccentric wife, Joy, in books such as
Bwana Game, *A lifetime with Lions*, and *My Pride and Joy: An
Autobiography*. His aim, it appears, was to narrate vividly the bonds
he forged with lions. The narrative that has lingered from these
movies and books—close to thirty years after he was killed—is that
of a selfless, adventurous white man who rescued lions and lived
with them for some time as he trained them for an unforgiving life
in the wild.

However, this is but a part of Adamson's life, attractively
crafted to give the man a larger-than-life image. Very little is said of
a man who killed animals for fun, traded in ivory, and even tried to
sell hunting safaris to clients, who failed in nearly all of the
businesses he attempted once he arrived in Kenya in the early
1920s, and who took a post in the game department in 1938 to
escape his many failures. He tried and failed in selling goats,
running a mail service, farming beeswax and honey, working as a
labourer on a sisal plantation, a barman, and a gold prospector, and
battling the Mau Mau freedom fighters. The man also took up a job
as a locust control officer but was sacked and also failed in road
construction after finding it too hard. By the time he was thirty-
two, Adamson had run out of finances. So, he took up a post in the
game department where he was assured of a life of adventure and
long years of idleness or little activity, which he supported through
fund-raising. He swam in global adulation for doing nothing
meaningful as far as actual conservation is concerned. This excerpt
is from *The Christian Science Monitor*:

> The photos of an idle man sleeping next to Elsa, the lioness,
> greatly captured the imagination and fascination of many a
> people who bestowed Adamson with legendary status. Some
> ended up documenting his immensely inactive life in films and
> documentaries while he himself wrote newsletters on mundane
> (natural) activities of the animals he lived with and immense
> numbers of letters, some of which he used to seek financing.

Very little is said about the fact that, as a game warden, Adamson killed the lioness that mothered the first three lion cubs he and Joy adopted in February, 1956. But that the world went on to idolize Adamson even after all his failures and without any reference to the havoc he must have caused as he and fellow hunters killed animals for fun or when he contributed to the killing of jumbos as he traded in ivory goes a long way to show that the conservation praise singing evident in the West has little to do with reality. Apart from this, we find George Adamson's contribution to conservation significantly inconsequential; the act of saving a few individuals of a single species (that went on to die anyway) through donor funding is neither here nor there. In conservation terms, it was largely a useless endeavour that served merely to romanticise wildlife, create an underserved heroism, and bailout a man who had failed in life by allowing him to rely on the mercy of donors. Adamson, though, believed he was up to some good. In some of his writings, it is evident that he saw himself as somewhat imperative to the survival of the animals he stayed with. Before he died on August 20, 1989, he wrote in *My Pride and Joy*:

> Who will now care for the animals, for they cannot look after themselves? Are there young men and women who are willing to take on this charge? Who will raise their voices, when mine is carried away on the wind, to plead their case?

Others took the glorification of Adamson further. He soon became *Baba wa Simba* (The Father of Lions). This man, who was not taken seriously by most scientists, has variously been described as one of the greatest conservationists of all time, "a man beyond his time," and "a hero whose devotion to Africa's lions stands unparalleled." He was lionized as a man who "sacrificed his entire life for the preservation and wellbeing of the endangered lions of Africa; battling against poachers, bandits, bureaucracy, and his own frailty of age just to preserve the habitat—the fauna and flora—of Kenya's untamed wilderness."

As Africans, we see this shrill praise as coming from the perspective of a people removed from the reality of wilderness in Kenya and elsewhere in our continent. To such people, the wilderness is a fascinating place full of adventure, promise, and danger in equal measure. Any white person who can dare to confront the wilderness (never mind that most live in extreme luxury afforded for them through the love and compassion that citizens of Industrial countries have for wildlife) must be a hero. Some in the praise choirs have a disturbing sense of geography; these are people who equate Kenya with all of Africa, often voicing views that are outlandishly ignorant. For such people, anything that comes from the mouths and pens of selfless white people working in Africa is to be believed. It does not matter whether what these heroes and heroines say are lies painted in attractive prose. This is the mentality that attributes Adamson with saving lions in Africa; the facts that he and Joy only saved slightly over twenty lions in a population of several thousand and that they never did so away from Kora and Meru parks either do not matter or are seen as inconvenient details.

In certain cases, this hero worship is self-serving and quite lucrative for those who lead the praise choirs. For instance, some of the Adamsons' worshippers have gone on to capitalize on the image they have created of the man by starting elaborate fund-raising schemes in his memory. For instance, with offices in Britain, the US, Kenya, and Ethiopia and projects in fourteen other countries, the international wildlife charity the Born Free Foundation was formed in 1984 by two actors who starred in the movie *Born Free*, Will Travers and Virginia McKenna. The charity bases its programs and fund-raising on Adamson's work, while Big Cats Sanctuary, located in the US State of Tennessee, asks people to support the rescue of big cats in memory of Adamson. Others have capitalized on his legend to rake in huge profits from movies and television series about a man whose life's work and contribution to wildlife conservation in Kenya has remained largely unevaluated to date.

Fast forward within the bureaucratic circles in Kenya, the exclusive association of people of European descent with conservation is now taken to another level. It is evident that for decades whiteness has been the most important consideration whenever top government officials make decisions pertaining to conservation in general and the management of the Kenya Wildlife Service (KWS) in particular. For instance, since it was formed, the KWS has had a high turnover of directors, but the lingering image and person of Richard Leakey, a high school dropout, has continued to dance before the subconscious of a country reeling from all manner of social, cultural, and economic contradictions. Having served twice as the KWS's head in the 1990s, Leakey was later appointed the assistant chairperson of the wildlife body's board of trustees. But even after spectacular failures and obvious signs that his health had greatly failed him, President Uhuru Kenyatta went on to appoint Leakey the chair of the KWS's board of trustees. Although Leakey would like it known that he was pushed into the position, he and other conservationists—including Paula Kahumbu, the head of Leakey's WildlifeDirect—had overtly influenced Uhuru's decision by constantly lambasting the KWS and its former top brass for botching the antipoaching war.

Today, Leakey enjoys a near-unanimous adulation in the West that is largely based on unschooled, uninformed perceptions. The praise became a shriek shortly after he was involved in a plane accident in 1993 that was allegedly organised by his sworn enemies within the Moi government. Leakey aided the coming Leakey-ism when he joined hands with Virginia Morell to author the book *Wildlife Wars: My Fight to Save Africa's Natural Treasures* in 2001. The 352-page book is little more than a chronicled, aggrandizing tome littered with self-perceived bravery and justified by a long complaint about corruption and dangerous (native African) criminals hell-bent on decimating entire herds and packs of wildlife in Kenya. As Ian Parker, a colonial game warden who stayed on in

Kenya to enjoy old money and sun after independence, said in a review of the book written by John Mbaria in *The EastAfrican,* the way Leakey went about narrating his story seemed to suggest if he had not done what he said he did, there would not be anything left to conserve.

By the time he led Moi to light a bonfire that consumed ill-gained ivory worth 60 million Kenyan shillings, Leakey had already secured a legacy that remains unquestioned by all who adore him—even when they read reports that paint him in a not-so-rosy image. Leakey's life story is coloured by an extraordinary degree of personal hubris and gross overestimations of his own importance in the conservation arena. Even the title of his book speaks of saving Africa's natural treasures, contriving to reduce the entire continent to his own stamping grounds. Maybe the greatest sign of this almost comical belief in his own hype is the working title of a planned movie on his life, Africa, set to be directed by Angelina Jolie, one of Hollywood's top actors. However, to some, including a growing legion of local naysayers, the global adulation of Leakey's layman's entry into the world of wildlife conservation and his largely self-perceived gigantic role in saving species is based largely on misinformation and a lack of information.

Though it is said that Leakey waged a personal antipoaching initiative for which he suffered immensely, his true legacy has escaped any rigorous or systematic scrutiny. But as we shall see in subsequent sections, unpacking Leakey and a small cabal of exclusively white conservationists and conservation thinkers in Kenya provides a ready answer to the mess the country faces today in regard to wildlife conservation. The lingering effects of the contributions these personalities have made to wildlife conservation have never been evaluated; the inherently fallacious contradictions the cabal has created since the colonial period have never been put in the spotlight by the people (native Africans) who now live the situation. Largely, what this cabal has done is merely viewed through a prism of thickly veiled racist perception, which in wildlife conservation, is apparently more important than reality.

What the common narrative refuses to point out is that as the world glorified Leakey and fellow white conservationists, the comradeship that communities living in wildlife-dominated areas had with the animals waned.

No one questions the effects Leakey's fortress conservation approach and its reliance on boots and guns has had on the conservation crisis Kenya is going through today. Even such evidently straightforward matters as the consequences that Leakey brought on Kenya when he gave his brother Jonathan a long-running permit to strip Kenyan forests of the highly lucrative bark of the *Prunus africana* tree has been avoided. Jonathan Leakey capitalized on the indigenous knowledge held by members of different African communities who have used the bark of the tree for over 400 years to prevent prostate cancer to rake in hundreds of millions in sales to Bayer Pharmaceuticals. In addition, no one has ever stood forward to say anything that would attribute Leakey to wanton decimation of wildlife, even though it is widely known that he allowed a cropping experiment that was racist in design and that exclusively allowed white ranchers to kill what were deemed excess animals on their ranches for more than twelve years. This conspiracy of silence has pervaded, leaving the evaluation of why and how the KWS has floundered ever since Leakey sat at its helm in the 1990s, or twice on its board and influenced its operations from without, to people seen more as spoilsports or macabre detractors of a living conservation messiah.

The wildlife conservation narrative in Kenya, as well as much of Africa, is thoroughly intertwined with colonialism, virulent racism, deliberate exclusion of the natives, veiled bribery, unsurpassed deceit, a conservation cult subscribed to by huge numbers of people in the West, and severe exploitation of the same wilderness conservationists have constantly claimed they are out to preserve. How colonialism fits into the conservation narrative is not so obvious as it may seem. But the use and bizarre enjoyment of wildlife was greatly intertwined with colonial power structures. Many modern wildlife parks were initially hunting grounds set aside for British settlers, most of whom belonged to the upper class or royalty. The very act of setting aside these game parks disregarded African people's claims to the land. In many cases, the who is who in the colonial regime was allowed to destroy ecosystems with abandon. For instance, Governor Charles Elliot gave one Colonel Ewart Grogan a concession of more than 100,000 acres of forest some one hundred years ago. This commenced the destruction of ecosystems in a major way, leading to the loss of more than half of Kenya's indigenous forests by the time the country attained independence. But in most books, magazines, and ordinary discourse, this fact is conveniently kept out as native Kenyans are blamed for overpopulating the country and spoiling everything.

Arena of Intellectual Contests

Kenya's conservation sector, like in many other African countries, has been an arena for European supremacy contests that have largely ignored, or actively suppressed, intellectual input from indigenous Africans. This has gone on since the dawn of colonialism, with European thought systems and their understanding and misunderstanding of the interaction of Africans with natural phenomenon constituting the only basis for law, policy, and practice in most sectors of the economy. This is observed in many fields, including wildlife conservation, where the intellectual divide has mainly been about whether private citizens can own wildlife, whether wild species should be used for sport and pot or preserved for their sentient and sentimental value.

On the one hand, there are those who have always argued that wild species are beautiful, admirable creatures that are sentient and have intrinsic value. Though amorphous, the group is comprised mainly of white Kenyans who draw support from a mainly indigenous elite working for conservation and animal welfare NGOs. Its members subscribe to the school of thought that is rabidly against any form of direct use of wildlife and appear to borrow leaf from a strange cult in the West that romanticises wild and domestic animals and plants above humans—especially humans with wooly hair and dark skin. Those who subscribe to this school of thought are bound to shout "Murder!" at any suggestion that wildlife ought to be husbanded and used the same way humans husband and use livestock. Just like its antithesis, this group has recruited many native Kenyans and has carried the day since 1977 when Kenya's first president, Jomo Kenyatta, banned hunting in the country. The group's victory was witnessed when it marshaled immense support against the inclusion of hunting in a wildlife law that was passed in parliament in 2004 before being denied presidential assent later.

The antithesis of this group is the prohunting group that believes that wildlife in Kenya will only survive and recover if it is owned by white landowners and treated more or less the same way livestock owners take care of their herds and flocks. Composed mainly of big-time game ranchers with sprawling properties in Laikipia, Nakuru, and Machakos and their intellectual sidekicks, the prohunting group has obstinately labored to convince the country of the virtues of legalizing sport hunting. They have continued to cling to a situation caused by sleaze, incompetence, institutional laziness, and an unwillingness to implement policy.

This group has found justification for its prohunting stance from the unwelcome reality in which the country has continued to destroy (wittingly and unwittingly) habitats, populations, and entire species. The saving grace, the group argues, lies in allowing landowners to take care of the animals and to conduct hunting safaris on their lands. Although the philosophy out of which the state assumed a monopoly over the management of wildlife began with an attempt by the colonial government to deny Africans the right to hunt or use wildlife, the group sees no shame in how it intensively lambasts this monopoly.

Among the top thinkers in the divide is David Western, the founder of the African Conservation Centre, who has done extensive research focusing mainly on how wildlife, livestock, and humans interact. Authoring such books as *Natural Connections:*

Perspectives in Community-Based Conservation, Conservation for the Twenty-First Century, and *In the Dust of Kilimanjaro*, Western is credited with giving birth to the concept of Parks Beyond Parks for the purpose of promoting community conservation. But like most of his contemporaries, he could not escape the trap of blowing his own trumpet.

Throughout his career, Western has shown a marked eagerness of making the world recognise his contributions to Kenya's conservation efforts. In line with the practice of self-praise so common with many of the top white conservationists in Kenya and other parts of Africa, Western's *In the Dust of Kilimanjaro* is nothing more than a romantic, personal view of his own struggle to protect Kenya's wildlife and an intimate glimpse into his life as a global spokesperson for silent wild species and populations, as well as local people, whose voices the world loves to shun.

He begins his narration with his childhood adventures hunting in rural Tanganyika (now Tanzania) and goes on to describe how and why Africa came to hold such power over him. He gives a blow-by-blow account of his long years of solitary fieldwork in and around Amboseli National Park and says this led to his gradual awakening to what was happening to the animals and people there. Together with his acceptance of the local Maasai culture, he says this made him realize that without an integrated approach to conservation, one that involved people as well as animals, Kenya would lose wildlife forever.

Western spices his book with a personal dimension by giving an account of his friendship with the Maasai. But although he presents an intimate knowledge of the nexus between Africa's wildlife and people and advocates for continued coexistence rather than segregation between people and wildlife, his later work as the head of the KWS failed to adhere to this notion. Whether he was just voicing a populist outlook might never be known. His theory that wildlife conservation ought to balance the needs of people and wildlife without excluding one or the other appears quite attractive and acceptable, but his true beliefs emerged when fielding questions from Paul Raeburn of the Associated Press on June 9, 1996. Western, who spent long years studying ecology with a view of how wildlife can survive within a highly dynamic scenario, came out in support of sport hunting, saying that game ranching and private exploitation of wildlife were critical for the maintenance of wildlife populations outside national parks. He went on to castigate the ban of big game hunting in Kenya, saying that it "took away any use of wildlife as far as the local communities were concerned, and they became antagonistic toward wildlife . . . wildlife became even more of a loss to the landowner at a time when the land pressures were very acute."

This is logical but in a warped sense. It is characteristic of conservation intellectuals of the European mould who have been quick to give lip service to the cause of communities, yet they are well aware that communities' entry into what is euphemistically called *consumptive use* is problematic, full of contradictions, and unsustainable, if the cropping experiment carried out between the early 1990s and 2003 (and which we describe in a subsequent chapter) is anything to go by.

As former director of the Kenya Wildlife Service, Western was active in many areas of conservation, including community-based conservation, international programs, conservation planning, ecotourism, training, directing governmental and nongovernmental organizations, and public education. He later contradicted his support for community involvement in conservation when he came out in opposition to the Kenyan government's intention to remove the Amboseli National Park from state control and hand it to a local authority, the now defunct Ol-kejuado County Council, in October 2005. Though Western justified his opposition to the move by stating that the move did not abide by the law, what he did not say was that for a long time Amboseli was managed, as a national reserve, by the Ol-kejuado County Council before it was unscrupulously taken over by the national government during the reign of Kenya's first President, the late Jomo Kenyatta. The move took place in the 1970s and effectively removed Amboseli from local management.

It is interesting that Western did not see the contradiction between drumming up support for his Parks Beyond Parks concept and his opposition to a move that would have given local people access to water and other resources they had shared with wildlife in the park long before the national government took it over. In Kenya, national parks are managed by the KWS, a state agency, and are out-of-bounds for anyone else, apart from tourists.

David Western's stint at the KWS was quite dramatic, as he was ousted by then President Daniel Moi on May 21, 1998, to which he made remarks that his ousting had to do with his opposition to giving miners access to national parks and that Moi had "whimsically" discontinued his contract. Moi was to publicly voice anger over Western's remarks saying that he considered them "cheap." Moi nevertheless went on to reinstate Western after six days only to sack him permanently four months later. Since then, Western has removed himself from mainstream conservation politics and has only come out openly once, in 2005, to oppose the handing over of Amboseli.

But there were others, including the late Imre Loefler, who did not shy off from the raging wildlife-conservation controversies of the 2000s or antagonizing native owners and managers of wildlife resources. Though an outsider, Loefler was among those who held a lot of sway on how Kenya conserved and what it conserved. His very background shows that skin colour is a major qualification for one to have influence on Kenya's conservation effort—much more than specialization in any field related to conservation. The Hungarian national studied medicine, philosophy, and history in Germany, trained as a surgeon, and later moved to Africa where he taught and practiced surgery in a number of countries. The highly opinionated man, who liked to ride horses in Ngong Forest, was instrumental in the formation of the Ngong Road Forest Trust that ended up fencing off part of the forest and controlling how the local people, including the inhabitants of the Kibera slums, accessed it.

Those who supported Loefler's take on the ills affecting wildlife conservation in Kenya believed the man was a thinker (some called him one of "the finest thinkers of our time"). He was a consultant surgeon at the Nairobi Hospital beginning in 1975, during which time he doubled as an author, a public speaker, and a columnist with *Daily Nation* and *The EastAfrican* and other publications through which he penned controversy at every opportunity. But the aging man, who admitted he was intolerant, impatient, and opinionated, also took up wildlife conservation, an immensely popular pastime among the white elitist groups in Kenya at the time. He was an avid supporter of sport hunting and deployed his substantial rhetoric in an attempt to wither opposition to sport hunting in the country. He took up many writing and talking opportunities to remind Kenyans of the folly of unchecked growth in population, terming *overpopulation* as the greatest problem facing the country. For instance, in "A New Game Plan for Wildlife Conservation" he says, "The principal reason for the environmental destruction is unchecked population growth, the very phenomenon that has impoverished Kenyans and rendered most public services a shadow of their former selves."

Loefler also argued, with characteristic logic, that land owners hosting wildlife need to be allowed to own the animals, saying that they should take care of them just like livestock owners do. He was against the idea of photographic tourism, believing that it had not led to equitable sharing of benefits. He saw nothing morally wrong with killing animals for fun: "It seems that at last the post-colonial era is coming to an end. We shall have to greet the new era by preparing ourselves for paradigm leaps. One such leap is to think the unthinkable: that sacrificing individual game animals can lead to the thriving of the species." Unfortunately for Loefler, Kenyans remained skeptical of the true intentions of the prohunting lobby. By the time he succumbed to cancer in 2007, Loefler's immense rhetoric had not managed to convince the country to embrace sport hunting.

Besides Western and Loefler, one other notable white intellectual belonging to the consumerist school of thought is Michael Norton-Griffiths. This American intellectual deviates from the orthodox approach to conservation. After living and working in a number of countries across the world he rushed to London over the ripe age of fifty, earned a Master of Science, returned to Kenya, and sharpened his arsenal against orthodox and romantic conservationists.

His papers betray impatience with the likes of Richard Leakey, whose largely layman's approach to conservation has been the bane of conservation scientists and scholars in Africa. Norton-Griffiths goes on, paper after paper, to espouse the economic approach to conservation doctrine that downgrades wildlife to a consumer good whose survival, as well as the survival of habitats, depends on whether, and how much, they contribute to land owners and users.

Norton-Griffiths believes that this is the missing element in the approach Kenya has taken to wildlife conservation. His irritation with anything that does not support his economic-approach hypothesis is astounding; he believes that economic consideration is all there is to wildlife conservation. Wildlife, he constantly says, can only survive and thrive if it pays rent for the space it occupies in the African wilderness. He considers this rent in terms of revenues shared between public bodies and the cash those involved in private conservation accrue from photographic and hunting safaris. To some extent, this could be part of the answer, but for Norton-Griffiths, it is the only answer. His sense of intellectual entitlement is evident in the way he hurls economic theory and arguments against prevailing conservation practice and sociocultural norms.

Characteristic of the many papers Norton-Griffiths authors is his penchant for assigning a monetary value to life forms. Wildlife, he says, disappears because land owners are not getting as much money as they do from other uses. He goes on to espouse a properly packaged yarn that land owners have not been given an economic reason to make them accept wildlife conservation as a viable undertaking. Tourism, to Norton-Griffiths, does not pay as much economic rent as sport hunting. And because white land barons in Kenya have been denied the right to sell safari hunts since 1977, he says that they have become disinterested in wildlife conservation, if not angry, and have been converting increasing portions of their lands for livestock and farming, thereby leading to decline in wildlife and habitats.

Looked at casually, this sounds convincing, until one realizes that Norton-Griffith's intellectual input into the conservation narrative is shamefully shallow. Nowhere does he question the underlying scenario, nor is he interested in the juxtaposition between the past and the present injustices caused by conservation or how this has created the situation he so castigates. Nowhere in his theories or formulae does he attempt to factor in the prevailing conservation power structure that is an inherent function of the phenomenon he describes and rubbishes.

With this in mind, one is inclined to believe that Norton-Griffiths's economic approach to conservation has little to do with ushering in an acceptable conservation reality. He goes on to suggest that because Kenya's economy cannot adequately foot the conservation bill on its own, the developed world must chip in substantially if the country is to maintain the conservation estate on its behalf, "until such time as Kenya can afford to carry the burden itself." He names and shames any other approach that disagrees with the use of animals to satiate greed: "Environmental economists will have it that the benefits of conservation vastly outweigh these costs, not just the direct benefits from access fees and the like, but from all the other indirect benefits represented by existence values, option values, and ecosystem services, such as carbon sequestration. As a skeptical economist, I now doubt the reality of much of this."

The man shoots from the hip; his target appears to be any model that prevents the realization of the long-running and concerted efforts to make the obscene pastime of shooting animals for fun acceptable in Kenya. Norton-Griffiths betrays his intellectual cowardice by not openly stating where he is coming from, lest he expose his mercenary tendencies and the identities of his financial backers. Rather, he goes around the issue as he takes intellectual detours that hide his real intentions. Like a literary night runner, he keeps dashing forth, brandishing some economic theory here, some mathematical formula there, and self-serving statistics all over to make the case for sport hunting. His true mission is to make the world believe that wildlife in Africa can only survive if the ultra-wealthy from affluent countries are allowed to spend top dollar killing it.

To Norton-Griffiths and his adherents, wildlife is only good if it can pay for its upkeep. What he conveniently refuses to say is that most of his papers (which he authored at a time when the hunting debate raged in Kenya) were meant to persuade authorities to allow those with money they cannot use in several lifetimes to roam all over the wilderness searching for the next lion to kill. Like many of his contemporaries, he is audacious and never burdened by self-doubt; though he does not demonstrate even a passable understanding of the cultures, world views, and philosophies of the indigenous subjects of his theories, he forges ahead to subscribe an economic approach for the conservation of animals on their lands. And he does not stop there.

Norton-Griffiths goes on to use the Western yardstick to expound on his understanding of poverty in native communities and believes that the world should not, for example, expect the Maasai to remain poor so that the last remaining herds and packs of wildlife on the planet can be preserved. He fails to factor or indeed understand why the Maasai, left on their own, would want to live and let wild animals live. Then he takes on the increasing population of Africans. Using high-sounding arguments and subtle intellectual nuances, he lampoons the womb and the children it brings forth for displacing wildlife and believes that, if adopted, economic considerations would stem the damage the womb has rendered on wild species and populations. The danger in this argument can be seen in the frequency with which the word overpopulation is used in the discourse around conservation in Africa, but the word is almost never used in regard to Asia, the world's most densely populated continent.

Land, for Norton Griffith, has little other value apart from the economic. Evidently, he cannot bring himself to accept that the other values people (and particularly African societies) place on land (e.g., religious and spiritual values and comradeship with animals) could be viable justification for creating and maintaining space for wildlife. He criticizes the unholy conservation fraternity in Kenya and elsewhere in Africa for keeping the world glued to conservation approaches that do not make economic sense to him. On this, the authors agree with him; but we remain unconvinced that his papers constitute a serious basis for conservation policy and practice. We believe that together with the orthodox conservation lot, Norton-Griffiths has played his part in rubbishing and discouraging the adoption and marriage of indigenous thought systems and conservation ethics with modern conservation practice.

Consumed by blinding arrogance, Norton-Griffiths, as well as the romantic conservationists he so vilifies, have not come to accept that their intellectual footprint on wildlife conservation has failed. Rather, they are determined to continue on dishing out confusing intellectual input and high-sounding arguments to keep alive a long-running narrative on why conservation has continued to fail in Africa, not on how and why they themselves have failed Africa's centuries-old grand conservation effort. This lot is determined to continue asking the world to look elsewhere for explanations on why species have continued to be lost. But in light of the impending demise of entire populations, one is bound to ask, for how long will Africa and the wider world condone such deception?

The Crisis Remains

Away from these contests between people who favour different conservation approaches, the conservation sector in Kenya is in a crisis that nobody can currently question. This crisis and its numerous angles have captured the attention of millions of people around the world and command millions of dollars in support. The magnitude of this support is as amazing as the broad spectrum from which it originates, ranging from individual pockets to the government coffers of the USA, the most powerful country on earth. In comparison to most other crises that afflict our world, it is unique in that it is one that is seldom downplayed by any of the parties involved—indeed, extraordinary effort is put into maintaining it at fever pitch.

What is in question is the true nature of the crisis and, consequently, the ways in which we seek to address it. Most of what we hear is about poaching, the need to curtail wildlife crime, the need to bring poachers and their ilk to book, and related objectives. This somewhat reveals the true nature of the crisis, the lack of understanding among the masses, and the relentless effort among a small minority to maintain the status quo. Wildlife conservation is being communicated to all and sundry as some kind of war that must be fought, and it's supposed leadership is filled with those who are touted as having saved a certain habitat or species from what we are always told was certain demise. The heroes of this war are always portrayed as people who have made supreme sacrifices to dedicate their lives to the cause. Poaching is undeniably a part of the problem, but to the honest observer, it is a minor part.

The most important part of the crisis, and arguably the driver of all human dimensions to the crisis, is the alienation of local people from wildlife conservation. When the colonizers came to African countries, they brought with them the archaic feudal structures around natural resource management that were the norm in the societies they came from. As part of the colonization processes, lands were annexed, and those that weren't cultivated were turned into national parks. These national parks were created expressly for the recreation of the settler communities, and this entailed the immediate exclusion of locals.

This book examines conservation as defined by the relationships through which people in Kenya have sought to benefit from wildlife. It is therefore important to note that these relationships may not necessarily meet the strictest definition of conservation, which implies benefit to wildlife and biodiversity. To put this into context, it is important to clarify that there are three different schools of conservation at play, and the interaction between the three determines the success or lack thereof in our current efforts to conserve. Firstly, there is the relationship precolonial African societies had with the wildlife in their environment, which was then adulterated by the relationship that British imperial statesmen, soldiers, hunters, and settlers cultivated with that wildlife as they arrived to colonize Kenya and other regions of Africa. Secondly, there is the relationships that have been created by those whose stated mission is to preserve or conserve wildlife in order to reap certain benefits, which often include exclusive consumptive use.

The second definition of conservation, which occurred with the arrival of colonial settlers in the late nineteenth century, most accurately describes a telling intersection of factors from which we have been unable to escape thus far. Their efforts to conserve were steeped in the need to create colonies. This was the basic need to control territory and create their own model of wildlife management, or use thereof, within the confines of that control. Before hunting was finally banned in 1977, it was the primary use of wildlife that dominated the identification of conservation objectives and the creation of structures to achieve them. The settlement of British gentry in Kenya brought in new norms of wildlife use. As elegantly described by Edward Steinhart in his book *Black Poachers, White Hunters*, there were attempts to "recreate on African soil, with African prey, the practices and values of nineteenth century European hunts complete with their class-ridden meanings and messages."

The geographical and temporal transplantation of these practices and values from feudal Europe resulted in the inclusion of two fundamental new values: Firstly, the class divide was instantly replaced by a racial divide. Here, nobility (read: privilege in the conservation and use of wildlife) was suddenly no longer conferred by lineage but by race—incidentally a fair proportion of settlers were soldiers and tradesmen from the lower echelons of British society. The cursory sharing of wildlife privilege that occurred in feudal Europe to maintain loyalty from the proletariat was no longer necessary in this colonial dispensation, so the hoi polloi from Britain embraced their new-found nobility with the alacrity of starving men thrust upon a banquet. Secondly, the context of colonialism gave conservation interests and newly minted gamekeepers the required impetus to define wildlife management or conservation through the prism of control of lands and all the resources therein.

Crisis is defined as a time of intense trouble, difficulty, or danger. It is therefore imperative that we define what exactly is in danger if we are to find ways of directly addressing or averting the crisis that African conservation now finds itself in. What is it that we stand to lose in the worst case scenario, that value that we must commit so much energy and resources to defend? This question elicits a wide variety of responses from different quarters and in many ways defines our perceptions today of what is considered to be the practice of conservation in East and Central Africa. This is the point at which the undue influence of the tourism industry is brought to bear on the conservation sector in East Africa. The tourism industry in East Africa grew largely out of the curiosity and fascination that British settlers found with the abundant megafauna they found in their new colony. There was also the romanticism, heroism, and self-actualization that was achieved through the conquering of these charismatic animals. This made Kenya a favourite playground for the rich and famous the world over, and the humble Kiswahili word *safari* became globally recognised as the epitome of wildlife-based recreation, encompassing both the photographic and hunting codes.

The combination of tourism's high profile as an earner of foreign revenue with the international reach of its partakers and practitioners moved this simple business from being a by-product of conservation to being the very basis for it. The importance of wildlife to Kenya and the communities herein has been reduced to the dollar value that foreign tourists will pay to see it. The cacophony over the importance of tourism earnings and the need for appreciation from our traditional source markets has drowned out the sense of ownership and cultural importance that indigenous Kenyan societies traditionally attached to the wild animals with which they share their environment. This is the crisis in which we find ourselves.

The keen student of conservation policy and practice in Kenya will see that this set of circumstances has resulted in foreigners and their wants taking all precedence over the need of locals in conservation decision making. This is particularly true in the vast unprotected wildlife habitats in the rangelands of northern Kenya. Civil society initiatives to structure conservation in these areas consistently include the formation of conservancies that exclude locals from core areas set aside for tourist use. The sheer amount of Western donor funding being invested in this model of conservation is an indication that a romanticized image of the African wilderness still holds sway across the world. One of the key questions we ask in this book is how are local Kenyans expected to accept and nurture wildlife that institutions and agents have worked so hard to alienate them from for over a century?

Further observation of conservation practice in Kenya shows that the monetary value of our wildlife is shifting from tourist earnings to donor funds. Donor funds are monies earned from selling ideas around a species or habitat. There is no product or service delivery as there is in tourism. True to form, several tourism outfits in Kenya and northern Tanzania have suddenly become conservation organizations. Here, we still pay for the unhealthy influence of tourism over conservation, because all these new outfits are run by foreign individuals and entities, few of whom are qualified to do so. But, if we look specifically at wildlife tourism in Kenya, we find that donor funds far exceed the earnings of this industry. In totality of the sector, the money earned by all forms of tourism in Kenya may exceed the amounts of donor funds, but in terms of how the money is used or distributed, there is no comparison.

It is our hope that this book will unmask the true challenges that threaten the existence of Kenya's wildlife and our ownership of our natural heritage. We have tried to present these arguments through the prisms of our individual studies and experiences and, whether or not the reader agrees, it is our hope that this work will stimulate debate, study, and discussion around the fate of Kenya's priceless natural heritage.

2 ~ Conservation NGOs' Grand Delusion

Manipulation of communities: Mordecai Ogada and Matei Koromo
working on the foundation of Esiteti school in 2008 under the aegis
of the Kenya Wildlife Trust. This school and water supply were built
south of Embarinkoi hill in an attempt to move the villagers and
their activities behind the hill, out of the view of tourists in the
Kitirua area and at Tortilis Camp. (©Mordecai Ogada)

The Green Man's Burden: The Cost of the Conservation Model Practiced in Kenya's Drylands

*In July of 1950, the Maasai of Amboseli agreed to lease fifty square kilometers
of land to the Royal National Parks to be used to develop campsites for safari
parties visiting the 3,260 square kilometer Amboseli National Reserve, created
two years earlier. In the course of that decade, tourism rose fivefold. Soon after,
the Maasai were moved away from the Ol Tukai swamps of the Amboseli area
to make way for an expanding safari tourism business. Assuring the Amboseli
Maasai that alternative water points would be constructed, the colonial
authorities relocated them then reneged on their promise, to the indignation of*

both the local and international conservation communities. But many conservationists also blamed the Maasai for the crisis. "If it was not for their preoccupation with excessive numbers of useless cattle there would never have been a need for their relocation in the first place," they said. The Maasai had apparently brought the problem on themselves.

In the early 1960s, Amboseli was transferred from the Royal National Parks to the jurisdiction of the then Kajiado County Council. The Maasai were cajoled and often arm-twisted into ceding more and more of their pastureland to the parks. Tourism skyrocketed. By 1969, income from Amboseli accounted for 70 percent of the Kajiado Council's annual budget. The Kajiado County Council wanted more land. Deaf to local protests, they attempted to carve out another 500 square kilometers of land belonging to the Maasai to be used exclusively for wildlife and tourism. The council only changed course when rhinos began showing up dead in the park. The government then nationalised the park in the early 1970s. To this day, revenues from Amboseli go directly to the central government.

Much like its history, the present day reality of wildlife conservation in Kenya's drylands is littered with similar stories in which governments, conservationists, tour operators, and hoteliers, in league with local leaders, have created an elaborate infrastructure exclusively for tourism and conservation. The dilemma, in this age of political-correctness? How can the real owners of these lands be placated while being shunted aside? How can they be convinced that they are benefitting while being deprived of their resources?

The cast of characters in this operation has expanded. Along with the usual suspects—the bewildered pastoralist, the strong-armed government, and the ever-zealous conservationist—we now have roaming battalions of NGOs and agriculturalists in search of new lands. And Kenyan natives pose a clear and present danger to wildlife (please ignore the fact that it is because of a wildlife management ethic they developed centuries ago that others in the world now enjoy this vast heritage).

The answer to this problem? Perpetuate a wildlife apartheid. Separate the people from the animals. Create parks, conservancies, and wildlife corridors, construct fences, charge at the park gates, perpetuate laws that put the animals first and tucks communities away in some dusty policy document; give the damned poachers long prison sentences and stuff the prison keys into some pit latrine. Call this participatory management. If they protest too much, offer the carrot: the gifts of rapidly constructed and understaffed schools and dispensaries interspersed with unreliable boreholes. You could even promise—with little obligation to deliver—certain revenue sharing arrangements: 25 percent if you woke from the right side of the bed, maybe even a couple of jobs at your proposed hotel, lodge, or campsite. If problems persist (hunting for the pot, poaching, illegal park entry of pastoralists and livestock, that sort of thing), consult the KWS, the big stick, the fierce, green men at the back of the land cruiser.

In the beginning (circa early colonialism), the drylands were an arena of contesting visions. The older traditional vision lost out, herded into history's cupboard, shut away so that what remains is a stutter, a squeak. Its defenders were narrow men entranced by new titles (for example, the Paramount Chief, a rank given to indigenous African leaders by the British), vague assurances, and brandy and who had little regard for their people. Their bargaining chip? Land. Over half a century ago, they negotiated away the Mara and Amboseli. Today they sell off, privatize, and fence off chunks of communal land to the most available bidder. As their people's way of life dies in a dust cloud of derision and overgrazing, so goes pastoralism, a livelihood that, if recognised and properly managed, could be as valuable as tourism (ask Botswana), as well as inclusive, participatory in a way that wildlife conservation can never be, and perhaps not as psychologically debilitating as the image of a gaggle of old Maasai women hassling tourists to buy bangles for twenty Kenyan shillings at the Namanga border being shooed away by irritated immigration officials.

Propped up by millions from international donors and indifferent to the resentment their activities provoke among locals, the conservation community in Kenya, in league with a government hungry for tourist dollars, has continued to advance a theory and practice of conservation that is almost unchanged since the days of Teddy Roosevelt. The difference, of course, is that saving the animals has replaced shooting them for sport. In other circumstances, its double standards would be laughable. Errant natives, whether they kill for protein or money, are called poachers. Their kill is called bushmeat. KWS rangers are trained to shoot them on sight. On the other hand, with the right connections and money (a European accent is also recommended), you can purchase a slice of the wilderness, call it a game ranch, shoot the wildlife, sell that sizzling side of impala for tourist dollars, and get away with saying that what you are doing is culling.

Conservation in Kenya alienates locals (pronounced w-a-t-u-s) from their resources—pastureland, dry season grazing areas, water points, and wildlife. It refuses to take any blame for the decimation of pastoralist economies, but it is very quick to take over the now empty lands with their silent population (watus can't read, you see). In place, it promises the locals a new source of income, a postmodern tourism (please try and clean up before you leave).

On a good day, this conservation will deliver a pittance of the revenues initially promised, gloss over this ancient deception with some slick marketing, and call it community-based conservation, partnership with communities, a grand new idea. For details, ask the well-meaning types with friends and email contacts in the West who buy and lease huge tracts of land for a song, sign management agreements with ignorant communities, control all the revenues, and claim that the real beneficiaries are the communities whose lives have been changed forever. In one case, a project spokesman proudly announced that the recipient community of 1,500 had earned one million Kenyan shillings ($11,756) in just eight months. Astonishing, this new income where none previously existed. But get your calculator, and that handsome sum translates to 666.60 Kenyan shillings ($7.80) per person over the period, or eighty-three Kenyan shillings (one dollar) per person per month. One dollar every thirty days. Ecotourism. Community-based conservation. Respect for local cultures.

Another reason for the enduring nature of Kenyan conservationism is that it is an end in and of itself. Save the elephants, sure, but besides the donor dollars, moral high grounds, and even sometimes genuine love for the animals, there is something about the romanticised way of life that will always attract a certain personality. The rhythm of life in the bush: Wake up early, ignore slight hangover, don khaki shorts and heavy boots, and head out into the bush. (Always remember to carry a sandwich lunch, and take Wariahe, an excellent Somali tracker acquired years ago. His sense of direction is amazing.) Scan the vast terrain for signs of night poaching. Why in God's name don't these people care? But it's not as bad as it used to be, the unbelievable holocaust of jumbos, the forests of snares. A ray of hope—the younger generation now appreciates animals and what we are trying to do here. It's really all about education. Shout. Cock gun. Arrest poacher, the bastard. Instruct Wariahe, bow, arrow, and simi (sword) in hand, to watch over the disheveled, downward-staring fiend. Radio the KWS to take it up from there. Eat lunch with back against the bonnet of Queenie, intrepid green, second-hand Land Rover of so many adventures. Spot leopard. Nip in at village centre to monitor progress of community women's ecotourism and dik-dik conservation project. Make impromptu speech. Mental note: got to improve the Kiswahili. Arrive at HQ-cum-home. Finish off the borehole project proposal (Preface: the plight and bent of the community women. Invoke image: dusty yellow jerricans strapped to their backs. Conclusion: this project will no doubt alleviate . . .). E-mail proposal in time for sundowners at Elsie's Pub (with its Jacks, its Gillians, and haven't-seen-you-in-a-while-Lyalls and its Jumas hovering darkly, smiling white-teeth smiles). Isn't the view from here simply splendid, my dear? It overlooks the salt-lick plain at the foot of the zebu-hump (in Maasai) hills. If you are lucky, you'll see giraffes lying down. Travel to town once a month for supplies and a peek at the savings account. Fly to London or Geneva or some atrocious American city very occasionally (it's important not to lose touch) to deliver paper on elephant dung counts. Consider writing Africa memoirs when the time comes, in late middle age, from a laptop in the London flat, nursing incipient arthritis. Dedicate it to Wariahe (double-check spelling), a dear friend once in Africa.

I am aware that conservation NGOs and foundations might take offence. Has the baby just ended up with the bathwater? Perhaps. But in my view, conservationism has never questioned the power structures in which it exists. It has assumed that government sanction and bribery will hide the resultant apartheid that stretches back a hundred years. Normally opaque to public scrutiny, when conservation is questioned, it justifies its existence with self-generated before-and-after statistics and intriguing scenarios (the history of elephant dung counts), with save-the-animal propaganda, with celebrated international campaigns, with the benefits of tourism. But at what cost?

This is a war between the self-proclaimed protectors of the wild and its owners, and there are no winners. New initiatives suggest that the way forward is further exclusion, adopting a neoliberal discourse (privatize, privatize, privatize) to a philosophy that has always depended on authoritarianism (conservationists have rarely objected to an African government with a firm hand and a sentimental streak). In the early 2000s, the big thing in conservation circles was the privatization of environmental resources. State corruption and incompetence provided powerful justification for this. Thus, DIY conservation. Then Ngong, a forest on Nairobi's outskirts, having been secured from land-grabbers, was handed over to the caring hands of a very concerned group of citizens. Having kept the kleptomaniacs at bay, the group quickly identified a new problem: slum dwellers, especially residents of Kibera, who had lived next to the forest for years (without destroying it). The way the conservationists went about it, one could be forgiven to think that the slum people were planning to clear the forest and put up Spanish villas. So, fence off the forest, hire and train some guards, then gentrify it. Transform it into a middle-class Garden of Eden. Charge at the gate, collect revenues for maintenance and staff salaries. It may be an idea to give the slum citizens ID tags so that the good ones can come in, at designated times, and collect wood (Remember, Juma, Philistina, only the dead wood, okay?).

There are many similar initiatives in the pipeline. How does this exclusion sit with that grand idea, the mission statement of conservation, safeguarding the wild for the unborn? At the rate things are going, will the unborn be able to afford to benefit from the wild in any way? And don't say that's just the point, that's why you are doing what you are doing today. Because as far as you are concerned, when you first arrived in Africa—that figment of your imagination—there was nothing, absolutely nothing, and in Africa there are two kinds of people. There are those born to fix the world's problems in time for sundowners at the club. Then there are the rest, those who just breed too much and spoil the view.

~John Mbaria (2003)

The illustration above is fictional and does not refer to any real individual or particular organization. It provides, however, an accurate and worrying snapshot of the Kenyan conservation scene outside protected areas where NGOs, rather than statutory authorities, tend to hold sway. The origins of these NGOs vary, but they all bear resemblance to that in the illustration, where an individual or a narrow shared set of interests gives rise to an organization. With the financial inflows that typically follow, these organizations grow exponentially, as does their reach, but they invariably suffer from their inability to depart from the ideas and visions of their founders.

The key question here is whether this tendency is necessarily a bad thing. This question raises strenuous arguments for and against NGO founders, because they are custodians of very creative and courageous visions but are no less vulnerable to the vices of avarice, hubris, and self-serving corruption than the rest of us. The positions for and against the retention of founders' influences in conservation organizations completely miss the most important point. Conservation is not a status that is achieved but a principle that governs continuous, living processes. In living ecosystems and species populations, what was true and applicable in 1995 cannot be so in 2014, and the relevance of these initial visions diminishes with the passage of time. The argument simply fails to appreciate the natural and socioeconomic changes that occur in African environments and societies over time. And unfortunately, we find today conservation NGOs in Kenya and much of East Africa proudly stating that they are still true to the vision of their founders that were proposed in the early 1960s and 1970s.

Whatever the nature of their origins, and their various foibles, the truth about NGOs in Kenya is that they fulfill a vital role. They fill the yawning gap left by the intellectual and scholarly vacuum in Kenya's statutory conservation sector. They are the ones who speak on the behalf of Kenya to donors, and they state Kenya's case where our intellectual sloth leaves us voiceless. A case in point is the current spike in elephant poaching and ivory trade that has somehow morphed into a threat to global security. The plight of the African elephant and the ivory trade were the subject of a session of the US Senate Foreign Relations Committee on May 24, 2012. The one invited to address this august company and give Africa's perspective was not even an African. It was Dr. Iain Douglas-Hamilton, a British researcher working in Kenya. His testimony was detailed and moving, and as a solution, he requested (predictably) more money, more planes, more helicopters, and the

38

like for individual researchers and conservationists. The achievements and efforts of wildlife authorities were glaringly absent from his testimony. Rarely has the absence of intellectual input from Africans in the African conservation arena been so starkly exposed.

One of the most prominent and successful conservation NGOs operating in Kenya and various other African countries is the African Wildlife Foundation (AWF). A look at its origins, if not its current operations, is a study of how interested foreigners moved quickly to colonize conservation in Africa in the 1960s, even as the colonial order continued to unravel. The precursor of the AWF was the African Wildlife Leadership Foundation, founded in 1961 by Russell Train, a wealthy American big-game hunter and member of the Washington Safari Club. His cofounders (also members of the Washington Safari Club) were Nick Arundel, Maurice Stans, James S. Bugg, and Kermit Roosevelt Jr. of the CIA. This illustrious group of founders set the AWLF apart from other conservation start-ups because they began from a position of significant financial strength.

Russell Train was worried that with the advent of independence for many African nations, European park managers would be replaced by Africans in conservation work. He was particularly concerned when, upon independence in 1962, the government of Tanganyika ordered the 100 percent Africanization of its game service by 1966. He wrote that "the replacement of European staff by untrained, unqualified men spells disaster for the game."

He was obviously blind to the fact that the European staff who inspired so much faith were mainly demobilized World War II soldiers with little more as wildlife management qualifications than firearms training and time on their hands. Nevertheless, this vision resulted in the funding and establishment of the Mweka College of African Wildlife Management, which has trained (if not necessarily educated) over 4,500 wildlife managers (not scholars or scientists) from twenty-eight African countries and eighteen non-African countries. The institution and its alumni have played a major part in the colonization of conservation in Africa. And the AWF has continued to thrive, with an annual budget estimated at over $20 million as of 2012. Their mission and activities are well articulated by a highly professional communications team. They now have a more varied and contemporary agenda, well supported by several donors, but African conservational thinking continues to reap the fruits of the seeds sown so generously by its founders half a century ago.

The African Wildlife Foundation is not immune to the tactical errors and odium that can be brought about by creating a monster with huge overheads that needs to be constantly fed with donor cash. In 2011, a perfect storm occurred in Laikipia, Kenya. Daniel Arap Moi, the former president, was in need of funds to handle the onslaught as people sought legal redress for real and perceived misdeeds during his twenty-four year autocratic rule. A 17,000 acre ranch he had acquired in Laikipia under unclear circumstances and never developed, Eland Downs, was quickly put up for sale. The Nature Conservancy (TNC) at the time was looking to acquire land and a foothold in Kenya, which for some reason is a prerequisite for conservation relevance worldwide. However, knowing the political heat around land acquisition in Laikipia, they needed a proxy through which to do so.

Enter the AWF, an NGO with a good reputation, political connections, and hunger for cash flow. TNC and the AWF came together and concluded this deal with a speed and alacrity that caught everyone off guard, except for the Samburu herdsmen who were using this land to graze their livestock. As soon as Moi's security personnel left, the Samburu quickly put up houses and settled. Later, AWF came to proudly survey their acquisition and were taken aback to find it a poachers' haven, occupied by people who were unwilling to move and their livestock.

The political machine at the AWF swung into action, quickly offering to give the land to the Kenya Wildlife Service for the purpose of conservation. The KWS, for its part, is always looking for land to enhance the size and connectivity of wildlife habitats. A brief ceremony at Harambee House, the office of the president in Nairobi, was arranged in order to hand over this gift, and it quickly became what is now known as Laikipia National Park. The KWS then quickly moved to take control of their gift the best way they know: boots on the ground, huts aflame, and gunfire in the air.

At least two people were confirmed dead, and there were allegations of numerous other rights violations by security forces, including beatings and rape. Human-rights and community-rights activists leapt into the fray promptly and with extravagant claims, including one that Eland Downs was once part of the Samburu herdsmen's ancestral land, never mind that the land is far south of Samburu and was privately owned prior to this latest acquisition. Over four years later, we are yet to see the end of the legal arguments or the public relations cloud cast by this blunder.

Towards the other end of the NGO spectrum, there are the NGOs that are local and have missions that are defined by narrower geographical horizons in addition to the founders' own limitations. The relative narrowness of their focuses allows these NGOs to be much better than their larger counterparts at actually solving real conservation problems on the ground. A narrow focus, however, can also result in untold difficulties when trying to grasp the larger conservation picture.

A case in point is the Laikipia Wildlife Forum (LWF). This organization was founded in 1992 by a group of large-scale ranchers in Laikipia District in central Kenya with the sole purpose of allocating quotas of zebras to be cropped for the sale of skins. This was an experimental partnership between the KWS and the landowners aimed at earning regular profits from the significant wildlife populations on their holdings. Even at this early stage, narrowness of vision showed through in the belief that consumptive use of wildlife could be carried out on certain privately held lands while being proscribed among the neighbouring communities.

This situation was not in any way helped by the fact that all the landowners involved in this experiment were white and all the neighbouring communities were black. After this zebra cropping was found to be unsustainable around 2001, the LWF moved into tourism development and destination marketing with various tourism facilities engaging in corporate social responsibility initiatives to uplift their neighbours' livelihoods. These included the development and equipping of schools, boreholes, cattle dips, and clinics.

The success of tourism in Laikipia coincided with the worldwide emergence of a strident paradigm stating that communities (read: black Africans) must earn money from wildlife in order to conserve it. This paradigm never explained why wildlife survived for millennia in Kenya's rangelands together with people who never earned anything from it, consumptively or otherwise. Nevertheless, it resonated with donors all over the world and resulted in strong support for anyone who espoused the lofty ideal of creating appreciation for wildlife among black Africans who would otherwise decimate this precious resource.

The Laikipia Wildlife Forum therefore grew into a strong and respected organization under this paradigm, even going further to create community-owned and -run tourism facilities, furthering their inclusion narrative. However, as with most myths, the inclusivity myth of the Laikipia Wildlife Forum was ruthlessly exposed from a totally unexpected quarter.

In 2011, the Kenyan government embarked on the development of a powerline to supply electricity to the Kenya grid from Ethiopia and routed said line through Laikipia. The core LWF membership (read: white landowners) protested vehemently against the project, often with more shrillness than reason, raising all manner of perceived negative impacts. These included the aesthetic, the economic (negative impacts on their businesses), and the ludicrous (construction of access roads opening up Laikipia to poachers and the line interfering with wildlife migration).

Selfish interests were shamelessly raised above national interests, billionaires claimed compromise of their livelihoods, and with this went the façade of community interest that the LWF had upheld for two decades. As the proverb goes, at a meeting of antelopes, the wooden horns failed to disguise the dog who snapped at flies.

Somewhere in between the international AWF and the local LWF lie regional NGOs like the East African Wildlife Society and Nature Kenya, formerly the East African Natural History Society. These organizations have been around for a long time, founded in 1961 and 1902 respectively. For a long time, both were important repositories of conservation knowledge in East Africa, but weak internal structures left them heavily dependent on the interests, skills, and leanings of their more charismatic members. It is therefore difficult to identify any strategic plans in the way these institutions operate, and they have eventually ended up following the money as they subsist from grant to grant.

These two NGOs are now involved in that amorphous activity known as advocacy, through which they have constantly discussed, supported, and sought other people's opinions without having any coherent direction of their own. The East African Wildlife Society, in particular, regularly underlines the elitist side of conservation by holding regular talks in Karen and Muthaiga, two of Nairobi's most exclusive members clubs, but maintains *Swara*— still the most important wildlife publication in the region.

The almost constant perceived crisis situation in conservation has also spawned personal NGOs that grow from a single person's activities or vision, usually in the conservation of a single species. In Kenya, the most prominent of these are Dr. Iain Douglas-Hamilton's Save the Elephants, Dr. Cynthia Moss's Amboseli Elephant Research Project, Dr. Joyce Poole's Elephant Voices, Dr. Max Graham's Space for Giants, and Dr. Daphne Sheldrick's David Sheldrick Wildlife Trust. These five examples together account for tens of millions of dollars in funding annually, but none of them actually tackle the problem of wildlife crime. It is also worth noting that they are all focused on one species: *Loxodonta africana*. A question well worth asking in Kenya is which sector makes the most money per elephant in Kenya—the government, the poachers, the tourism investors, or the conservationists?

Money follows stated intentions. Often stated in mission or vision statements, the NGO's hunt for donor cash starts after a selection of catchy, attractive, and widely used buzzwords that resonate well in a world that stands accused and—to some extent—feels guilty for being unable to live and let other residents of the planet live. The words used are usually in sync with the latest global conservation fad; they must also be in line with a philosophy crafted in the West about how Africa ought to be aided to protect its own wildlife, a global resource.

NGOs also find a need to be obscure and sophisticated as they clamour for the almighty dollar. In this regard, rather than simply say that they are opposed to the killing of wildlife by land owners who host it, many find it sexier to put on paper their opposition to any form of "consumptive utilisation of wildlife." And when it comes to the act of taking guns, loading them with ammunition, aiming at hapless animals, and pulling triggers, NGOs talk of cropping, culling, or sport hunting—whitewashing a bloody undertaking by those who believe they hold life-and-death rights over animals.

From its face, this penchant for obscurity appears like a minor thing. But when considered against the fact that the personnel of many NGOs usually act on behalf of exogenous and inordinately Western commercial interests that have never shown any interest in preserving Africa's wildlife, then their implication in species disappearance becomes apparent. Before they are allowed to reap from its largesse, before being accepted in the West, NGOs working in Kenya must fulfill certain written and unwritten rules.

For one, they must be seen to toe the line taken by their counterparts in the West. They must constantly keep tabs on the pursuits taken up by large conservation bodies, including different agencies of the United Nations, the Bretton Woods institutions (the World Bank, the International Monetary Fund, etc.), and the international foundations that finance conservation in Africa.

Conservation NGOs must also be seen to toe the racial line; one can only succeed in the NGO world if they are white or have a close and preferably familial or business affiliation with one or more members of the Kenyan white community. Starting an American chapter or getting an American to sit on the board is an added advantage.

Substance is not important. An NGO stands to reap more by being seen to be as loud as possible, the thinking being that if the media notices you, you must be doing something right and, therefore, deserve a constant flow of dollars. In most cases, if you can meet these and other conditions, you do not have to do what you say; you only need to be articulate. If you carefully state your intentions, the dollars will be yours for taking.

It is with this in mind that small, shaky, and highly personalized NGOs have been started—many by daring Kenyans who do not miss any sleep as they pronounce what they cannot possibly attain. These include the Africa Network for Animal Welfare (ANAW), an organization that has stated in copious documents that it is about the promotion of the humane treatment of all animals, biodiversity conservation, conservation education, good agricultural practices, and habitat protection without ever stating its geographical areas of operation.

Formed by Josphat Ngonyo, a hyperactive, somewhat incoherent fellow, the ANAW's mission and vision are crafted along the same lines adopted by the International Fund for Animal Welfare. With seventeen dwindling members of staff as of 2012 (a majority of whom were recruited from local churches and Bible-study fellowships), an office in Nairobi West, and a campsite at Kasigau outside Tsavo East National Park, ANAW does not have the required capacity to do what it says. But the organization's size and capability is eclipsed by its presence in the media with Ngonyo, a B.A. alumnus from Moi University, actively seeking any available media opportunity to pontificate on many issues—wildlife law, genetic engineering, good agricultural practice, factory farming, species diversity, community conservation, habitat protection, and so on.

The ANAW and Ngonyo the man are symbiotic entities. Without Ngonyo, the ANAW would cease to exist. Ngonyo started the ANAW in 2006, soon after being kicked out by the board of Youth for Conservation, another organisation he launched with his bosom friend, Steve Itela (who later became the ANAW's Director of Operations). Six years later, Ngonyo went ahead to personally appoint members of the ANAW's board, including his wife Agnes, after an earlier board led by a university professor, Charles Kimwele, resigned in its entirety, citing integrity issues.

But this has not deterred funders—particularly in Britain and the US—from bankrolling the organization. The saving grace for Ngonyo and the ANAW has been his connections with a member of Kenya's white community. Indeed, Ngonyo owes his entry and acceptance into the circle of Kenyan conservationists and link to British and American financiers to his adoption by the late Rosalie Osborne, as well as his later friendship with David Gies, an American fund-raising expert based in Denver who opened the ANAW-USA branch and at some point worked as the organisation's Chief Operating Officer in Kenya without a formal work permit.

In comparison with multi-national NGOs, such bodies like the ANAW cannot be said to be as harmful; their biggest crime is to mislead the world that so much is being done to protect wildlife in Africa while all they do is to live from one insignificant, (sometimes dubious), short-term activity to another in the hope of keeping donors interested.

While NGOs outdo themselves to please foreign financiers, most do not ordinarily adhere to the wishes of government bodies. They are able to circumvent, and at times alter, conservation policies and laws set by governments to suit their needs and the needs of their financiers or owners. This is largely because the institutions of governance in Kenya, for example, are not only characteristically weak but also incapable of enforcing policies or whipping NGOs into line. Their failure to run the national conservation show is made worse by the lack of a discernible conservation agenda, low budgets, poor pay to staff, a near-apathy toward efficiency, and the inability to quickly identify the full implications of their actions and inactions.

Added to these is the fact that members of Kenya's civil service, particularly those occupying the higher decision-making echelons, have largely forfeited their roles as policy makers. In many ways, they are no longer involved in setting up national conservation, social, economic, or political agendas. Occasionally, they do come up with elaborate blueprints, such as economic recovery programs or Kenya's Vision 2030 plan that lays out various targets for infrastructure developments, service provision, and economic growth. But on the whole, civil servants in Kenya have given up on their role and independence to determine how progress is steered in the country.

To a large extent, the mandate given to government departments and agencies such as the Kenya Wildlife Service, the National Environment Management Authority (NEMA), or even the Environment & Natural Resources Ministry to steer conservation along a more patriotic path has been usurped and corrupted by foreign interests working through local and international NGOs. It is very curious that the judiciary, under former Chief Justice Willy Mutunga, who previously headed the Ford Foundation in Eastern Africa, joined hands with NGOs, the police, and the Office of the Director of Public Prosecutions to craft a system of making effective the entire process of arresting, prosecuting, and sentencing convicted poachers.

Apparently, Mutunga and Joel Ngugi, his point man at the Judiciary Training Institute, did not see anything wrong with subverting the judicial independence of judges' and magistrates' parochial scrutiny as they allowed them to participate in the so-called national dialogue on wildlife crimes in 2014 and 2015. The sessions were funded by a plethora of donors through the ANAW,

WildlifeDirect, the Africa Fund for Endangered Wildlife Kenya Ltd., and Act Change & Transform (ACT!). The judiciary as a whole might not have allowed its role to be influenced by NGOs, but the fact that judicial officers of considerable repute would queue and sign for handouts from NGOs at the end of the sessions puts to question whether this very act did not end up compromising their objectivity.

In a nutshell, by allowing officers under him to be guided by NGOs, Mutunga called into question his ability to shrug off activism from how he managed one of Kenya's most important institutions. It also underscored the fact that nearly all institutions in the country, as well as most other aspects of Kenyan society, are now at the beck and call of foreigners through NGOs and other outfits.

The review process of the 1989 Wildlife (Conservation & Management) Act points to the dangers posed by this malaise. This piece of legislation gave rise to the Kenya Wildlife Service under Richard Leakey, but it had inherent contradictions that prevented the smooth operations of the KWS; it did not appreciate or cater to the roles that local people ought to play in conservation. But as Kenyans clamoured for a review of the act, rich private ranchers and others who hold onto the biggest slice of the proceeds emanating from conservation ganged up with NGOs to develop a bill that they handed over to one of Kenya's parliamentarians, Godfrey Gitahi Kariuki, who agreed to sponsor it as a private members bill in 2004.

The bill said very nice things about raising the amount of compensation paid to families of people killed or injured by animals. It also provided a rationale for the restructuring of the Kenya Wildlife Service. But hidden in its pages was a clause calling for the lifting of a ban on sport hunting that was put in place in 1977 by Kenya's first president, the late Jomo Kenyatta. This was the crux of the matter. Once again, NGOs led from the front. Although a number, led by the local chapter of the International Fund for Animal Welfare, were rabidly against the resumption of pleasure hunts in Kenya, many, led by the East African Wildlife Society, outdid themselves to ensure the bill was passed in parliament.

The United States Agency for International Development (USAID) was also instrumental in financing the process; the US agency expended 41 million Kenyan shillings ($482,352) to foot the cost of organizing meetings and paying consultants, one of whom was recruited from Zimbabwe. At some point, local NGOs ganged up with Safari Club International to finance a fully paid trip for Kenyan legislators, government officers, and media personalities to several southern African countries that had allowed sport hunting. As this blatant bribery was taking place, the esteemed World Conservation Union (IUCN) launched a project to showcase the virtues of sport hunting in the wildlife-diverse Samburu County.

Evidently, the big scheme here was to manipulate Kenyan law makers into appreciating the merits of sport hunting while frustrating the enactment of an animal-friendly law that could also recognise and reward the contribution local people make towards the survival of species diversity and the maintenance of ecological integrity in the country. Fortunately, then President of Kenya Mwai Kibaki refused to assent to the law after the act was passed on the night of December 9, 2004, by a small group of legislators. Kibaki cited the need to involve many more Kenyans and ordered the law to be redrafted.

Once the new review of the act commenced, the World Wide Fund (WWF) was among the NGOs that played an influential role in manipulating the process. The WWF is one of the largest NGOs with a multi-million dollar budget, a presence in one hundred countries, and close to five million members. And still the WWF felt it could not manage on its own. It crafted a strategy that involved putting together the collective voice of the conservation NGOs in Kenya by launching and bankrolling the National Environment Civil Society Alliance of Kenya (NECSA). It also footed much of the cost incurred by a technical committee that was appointed by the Kenyan government to guide the new review process. This committee mainly listened to the fraternity of well-to-do, white, large-scale private ranchers, NGOs, and everybody else apart from representatives of the local people who live with wildlife.

After a protracted process, through which different versions of the bill were drafted and shelved, the new act was eventually enacted in late 2013 and finally received assent from President Uhuru Kenyatta on January 10, 2014. The WWF admitted its role by saying that it "coordinated the input of environmental civil society organizations." And although the role of implementing new laws in Kenya is assigned to different statutory bodies, the WWF also claimed that it remained committed "to ensuring the full operationalisation of this act."

But what the WWF did not say in its communiqués is that some of its staff members were in the technical committee that met surreptitiously (often in luxury hotels) to determine the content of the new law, which is bound to have far-reaching implications on wildlife and community-wildlife interactions in Kenya. At some point, the committee refused to involve groups of local people who live in wildlife-dominated areas and who were totally against the legalization of wildlife killing. By denying local people the right to participate, the WWF and the committee contravened the 2010 Kenya Constitution that now provides for all-inclusive and consultative law-making processes in the country. But what most shocked many committed conservationists in Kenya, was that the new law allowed the killing of wildlife through cropping and for research. However, because it has a well-thought-out public relations campaign, most Kenyans could not associate such provisions with such a giant organization as the WWF.

Indeed, the WWF has largely managed to keep its dark past under wraps. And so, to most Kenyans, the organization has been nothing but a welcome saviour, an altruistic outfit that plays a crucial role in conserving the country's wildlife resources. To its credit, the WWF has attained mastery in publishing its deeds, which has kept it in good books with African governments and citizens. But being in good books with people who are ignorant of its history has not reduced the implications of its past actions (and inactions) toward Africa's wildlife populations and species diversity.

According to the Oxford-based academic Prof. John Phillipson as presented in *More Dangerous Ground: The Inside Story of Britain's Best Known Investigative Journalist* by Roger Cook, the WWF contracted a report on all its internal workings since 1961, and the organization is hardly the saintly outfit it portrays itself to be. Phillipson established that, even after spending millions of dollars, the WWF's flagship projects of saving the elephant, panda, and black rhino had failed miserably. Instead of working on big-impact, low budget projects, the organisation preferred to waste precious financial resources on grandiose conservation projects for which it had no hopes of success. For instance, the WWF injected £1 million to conserve pandas in China. But rather than use the cash to breed pandas, the Chinese used much of it to build a dam that flooded the panda's natural habitat.

Closer home, Phillipson revealed a secret report that exposed one of Kenya's most prominent families, as the chief organizers of an illegal ivory trade that was rampant decades ago. This was in the 1960s and 1970s when Kenya lost tens of thousands of its jumbos; the population has not recovered since then. Senior WWF officials, as Phillipson reported, knew about the involvement of these prominent personalities in the ivory trade, but they did not just keep quiet; they went ahead to 'reward' some with the Golden Ark, then considered the highest accolade for wildlife protection.

In Zimbabwe, Phillipson reported that the WWF provided rich white hunters with quarry: "The Charity gave out leaflets telling you which Zimbabwean game ranches to visit to join the hunt." He went on to describe, in considerable detail, how the hunts—which resulted in what can only be described as wanton destruction of Africa's most important heritage—were organized: "For a few thousand dollars, you could kill one of the WWF's cherished elephants." When Phillipson presented his report, the WWF suppressed it. The report remained under wraps until it was made public by Roger Cook, one of Britain's most famous investigative journalists. The secret was out, and the WWF could not hide it any longer. Even the attempt by its international president, the late Prince Bernhardt of the Netherlands, to accuse Cook of stealing the WWF's internal documents did not wash; its director at the time, General De Haes, resigned shortly thereafter.

In Kenya and elsewhere in Africa, the WWF's concept of *sustainable utilisation* is a mere euphemism for a scheme that has nothing to do with conservation; it is rather about assigning a cash value to wildlife species and allowing the rich and famous to kill them for pleasure. The stated goal is that the proceeds can be used to finance the survival of other species that will end up being killed in subsequent hunting escapades. Even with this elaborate window dressing, the stench of the rot of policy within the NGO occasionally breaches the cover.

The most recent instance of this is the removal of King Juan Carlos as the patron of the WWF in Spain after an accident led to the exposure of his July 2012 elephant hunting trip in Botswana. the WWF is in a league of big-time NGOs operating in Kenya that have, at on point or another, come out to support the reintroduction of sport hunting in the country. Their game plan has been to prime Kenya's considerably big populations of diverse wildlife for pleasure hunts. But because of a national tide against such killings, they have attempted to be subtle.

As our investigations show, some of NGOs have also been salivating over some of Kenya's other well-preserved natural resources. In most of these cases, the NGOs go on to claim that all they were up to was to ensure better management, if not sustainable utilisation. But when locals come out to oppose some of their high-sounding and well-hidden schemes, some do not see the irony of NGOs ganging up with ruthless administrators to force local people to play ball. Rarely, too, do such NGOs regard such coercion as inconsistent to what they profess in PR documents.

One instance that deserves mention is the saga surrounding an attempt by the IUCN to put in place what it termed a *modern management system* for the 33,000-hectare Naimina Enkiyio (or Loita) Forest in southern Kenya in 2004. As we investigated what the IUCN did, it emerged, yet again, that some big-bucks NGOs operating in Kenya and other countries in Africa have been rendering a hand to mercilessly root out local people from their lands. It all started with a phone call made to John Mbaria—who was then a reporter who many members of the white conservation fraternity in Kenya considered as taking an antagonistic position to their interests. The call came from Mbaria's Maasai friend Sammy Ole Mpetti, with whom Mbaria had toured Tanzania's Loliondo Game Control Area that is operated by Otterlo Business Corporation, a company with links to the royal family in the United Arabs Emirates.

"I am angry with what is happening at Loita," Ole Mpetti said in an agitated tone. He then pleaded with Mbaria to investigate the matter. Mbaria began by first making a detailed tour of the IUCN's website, which claims in part that the organization "operates in an increasingly complex world" where phenomena such as globalization and climate change mean "that traditional solutions and ways of working are no longer adequate to solve some of the challenges the region is facing in seeking to achieve sustainability."

The IUCN also claims that it builds partnerships with a broad range of actors and sectors, including public, private, and civil society "through equitable partnerships that enable and encourage a diversity of views, knowledge, and experience." But as the Loita saga unfolded, it emerged that this was not entirely true. Indeed, the IUCN's well-kept positive image in Kenya was sullied once it started working with local administration to forcefully take over the management of Loita forest.

This primed it for a conflict with the Maasai people, whose anger was accurately captured by the sentiments expressed by one elder during a demonstration against the IUCN on June 19, 2004: "The British moved us from Nairobi and Nakuru [in the early

1900s], but we shall fight current attempts to move us from Naimina Enkiyio." In an attempt to ensure that the IUCN's desire carried the day, the local administration deployed the police who characteristically beat up the locals. One person was killed and many were injured.

The three-year IUCN project was funded by the European Union. Aptly named the Loita/Purko Naimina Enkiyio Forest Integrated Conservation and Development Project, it was meant to complement the traditional conservation system employed by the Maasai and thereby aid in "maintaining the biodiversity and environmental values" of the region. The IUCN hoped the project would cover the entire upland forest lying between the Nguruman and Magadi escarpment and the Maasai Mara National Reserve. Straddling the Kenya-Tanzania border, this largely virgin forest has a wide diversity of vegetation and offers the local people not only timber and medical herbs but also sites that continue to be of cultural and spiritual importance.

As Mbaria dug into the matter, it became apparent that the saga typified a deceit that is so prevalent among many conservation practitioners in many parts of Africa. It also exposed a clash of cultures in that the Maasai people were determined to maintain a traditional conservation and management system that had worked well for hundreds of years. But it also exposed how deceptive NGOs can be.

In its budget, the IUCN planned to expend the lion's share of the $2.56 million EU grant to pay the salaries and allowances of its staff and to purchase and to maintain big fuel guzzlers and office equipment. In an interview with Mbaria, the IUCN's then regional programme co-coordinator for East Africa, Geoffrey Howard, saw nothing wrong with this as he defended the budget and the entire project saying that it was not "secretive" and had been prepared in accordance with the requirements of the financier. He admitted that the IUCN had contracted an expensive expatriate who was to bring "his international experience to the project."

But the local Maasai wanted none of it; they wanted the IUCN out, to leave them alone. "This is a forest we have always fallen back on in times of calamity and for medicine," said Vincent Ntekerei, a former lecturer at Narok Teachers Training College. "We do not know IUCN's real intention," another local, David Ole Kashu, said, adding that having managed the forest for ages, the community was opposed to what they felt was "outsider interference."

Several of those interviewed were members of a group of educated and articulate local residents who, operating under the auspices of Concerned Citizens of Loita, took the IUCN and the local administration head on. They went on to organise a public meeting during which speakers expressed their common view that the local Maasai should continue managing the forest "like we have always done for generations." They opposed the IUCN's proposed draft management plan and drew parallels with an earlier IUCN scheme that ended up displacing local people around Ngorongoro area in Tanzania in 1997 for the purpose of creating a wildlife sanctuary. Howard admitted this, saying that the latter project only became problematic after the donor reduced project time: "This led to one group not being consulted." He then went on to accuse the disgruntled group of producing a video and a report that "substantially damaged IUCN's image."

As the tale continued to unfold, many commentators could not understand why the IUCN appeared not to accept that it was because the local community had maintained strict traditional conservation ethics that Loita Forest had survived intact at a time when most other forests in Kenya—which were managed through a Western management philosophy—had largely lost their tree cover. In Loita, no local was allowed to cut down any tree without the consent of the Loita Naimiana Enkiyio Conservation Trust. Besides hosting sites that are still sacred to most members of the Maasai community in Kenya and Tanzania, Loita is the seat of the chief *laibon* (revered seer and spiritual leader), Mokombo Ole Simel, who is reputed to possess mystical powers and presides over social events in the area, including the community's forest management committee.

What took place at Loita puts to question whether the NGO movement in Kenya has truly been working for the interests of conservation. This debate was rekindled following the enactment and implementation of the Public Benefits Organizations Act of 2013. But the debate became so emotional that the real issues were lost in the melee. One thing is clear though: Africa has had more than its share of bad times. For so long, its growth prospects have been minimal while many of its people remain poor and desperate as preventable illnesses take millions to their graves.

As this has happened, the number and financial muscle of NGOs has grown exponentially. The perceived need for NGOs was authenticated by the fact that since Kenya and other African countries have attained political independence, they have suffered from all manner of ills—inter-tribal conflicts, massacres, official neglect, forest degradation, droughts that have risen in frequency and severity, loss of productive capacity, destruction of wildlife species, political assassinations, and so on.

In a place where deprivation ravages millions, and as traditional structures for resource sharing gave way to primitive accumulation and self-interest, it has become increasingly natural for the victims to view the NGO movement as the long-awaited messiah that would help to scour penury and hopelessness from every corner of the continent. And by broadcasting—and sometimes exaggerating—the extent of what they do, NGO officials have been complicit in bringing home the notion that they are the very prescription the doctor ordered for healing wounded ecologies, as well as righting the continent's socio-economic contradictions and soothing political upheavals.

But decades after the NGOs gained a foothold in Africa, such notions have come under constant interrogation. Conservation NGOs have not escaped this examination, with many questioning whether these foreign funded entities are about forging and sustaining Africa's ecological integrity or whether they have their own agenda. A similar question that has surfaced is whether what NGOs do (or say they do) is of any help for a continent seeking to find itself within the morass of a geopolitical equation that has long relegated it to the periphery of human development.

Foreign-funded NGOs have increasingly been regarded as entities that have been subtly working against the national interests and sovereignty of many African countries. This is not to say that there is a confluence of opinions on this issue. There are those who believe that because all governments—even the best of them— have structural weaknesses and inherent contradictions, they are unable to address most of the problems afflicting society. And those who say so might also assert that NGOs have been filling such gaps and are thus necessary for a developing hemisphere.

But a more potent criticism has been that the very foundation of Africa's civil society movement is alien. Those who raise this criticism accuse NGOs of continuing the work started by missionaries who ganged up with British, French, Portuguese, Spanish, and—to a lesser extent—German and Italian colonizers to control Africa and rob its resources in the name of protecting the same from unsustainable use by its natives. They accuse local NGOs and the entire civil society movement of been unwilling or unable to chart their own causes or to determine the nature of their activities or to align themselves with the struggles of local people as expressed by officially declared national and local economic, ecological, social, and political agendas.

The greatest predicament for people in Kenya and elsewhere in Africa is that they have unwittingly allowed pursuits that have little to do with the interests of the greatest majority to form the core of national development. Rarely do Africans ask questions such as why foreigners have felt it necessary to dish out lots of cash to protect wildlife or to prop up community conservation schemes. Rarely do questions occur like what use an economically emancipated Africa would be to foreigners who have historically reaped big from making vast parts of the continent poor and desperate.

Firoze Manji, author and former editor of *Pambazuka News*, says that the work done by NGOs contributes marginally to the relief of poverty but significantly to undermining the struggle of African peoples to emancipate themselves from economic, social, and political oppression. To Manji, NGOs by their very operations pressurize the society—through a variety of means—to comply with what he calls an "externally defined agenda for social development."

Other scholars believe that NGOs sustain an artificial, false economy that is not grounded locally. This is a position maintained by Abdul Ghelleh, who in *NGOs in Africa: Assets or Liabilities?* says that these groups push huge amounts of cash into the pockets of corrupted local African partners while still taking most of the cash back to their private bank accounts. To Ghelleh, NGOs actually work against home-grown developmental strategies in Africa. To a great extent, these arguments can be applied to all NGOs, including conservation NGOs.

Who are NGOs accountable to? Owing to the fact that African states do not directly fund them, states do not have a way of monitoring NGOs' operations. As a result, NGOs in Africa have continued to dish out situational reports to foreigners on every aspect of African societies. They have also gained almost unlimited powers, particularly because they have been minimally sharing with government officials and local people the largesse extended to them by foreign financiers.

It is out of this scenario that countries such as Kenya have been passing laws and enacting policies pushed through by foreigners through NGOs. To some extent, this includes the Wildlife (Conservation & Management) Act of 2013. Although wildlife viewing generates 70 percent of the foreign exchange earnings Kenya receives from the tourism sector, as detailed earlier, a well-orchestrated scheme by game ranchers who worked hand in hand with the WWF, IUCN, Safari Club International, and USAID led to a wildlife law that allowed for the killing of wildlife through sport hunting. And even after President Kibaki ruled out the resumption of hunting, the ranchers were able to push through such practices as cropping, culling, and killing wildlife for research in a subsequent law.

Although local people have subsequently been fighting against such provisions in Kenya's wildlife laws, it is not clear why NGOs have continued to support what could have ended up finishing off the goose that lays for Kenya the golden egg. This calls for a review of the role and power wielded by NGOs in Africa. Although they have a role to play in any society, they should never be allowed to become too powerful; they should never be permitted to become an alternate to government. African governments should work hard to bring NGOs to heel. And if power is with the people, then any movement ought to be subjected to the laws agreed upon by society.

One specific area that needs to come under scrutiny is how NGOs have been hoodwinking Africa to preserve its resources while at the same time working closely with companies in the West who are deeply involved in exploiting those resources. This is authenticated by the story of the African violet. As we investigated this story, we came across a subtle scheme whose details have somehow escaped the media's spotlight—instead the media consistently goes to the street with another story crafted directly or indirectly by the NGOs. Usually, the story starts with a selfless party and a dream to travel to Africa and help save one or more species from destruction by the local people. We cite the case of the African violet to expound on the fact that, while Africans are typically encouraged to conserve nature, the West is actively engaged in commercially exploiting it. To us, the effort to save the last wild population of African violet in Kenya is a story that outlines the predictably paternalistic trajectory.

The African violet is found in the 400-acre Mbololo Forest in the Taita Hills in Kenya's Coast Province. This is also known as a cloud mountain forest whose steep terrain is usually bathed in cloud and has moist habitat that is home to a great many plant species. Growing on cliffs and large rocks under the forest canopy is the last remaining wild population of the *Saintpaulia teitensis* species of African violets.

The area adjacent to the forest has a rapidly growing human population, with people engaged in an intense daily struggle for survival. Entire families toil for long hours to make little more than two dollars a day. But few people in the community are aware that the African violet—a plant with thick, leathery dark green leaves with red undersides that bears four to eight bluish flowers—is more than a just a pretty flower, that cultivating it on a commercial basis may hold the key to what they need to break from a cycle of poverty.

Strangely, those who are aware of its economic and aesthetic potential have been working hard to save what they term the *last frontier* of the African violet. No one has bothered to educate the Taita people on the fact that the flower can literary change their lives. Indeed, our investigations revealed that the Taita people appear to be in the way, and the persuasive power of the dollar is being brought to bear to get the Taita to look elsewhere for income-generating activities, so that they will no longer use the forest's resources intensively, thus contributing to its preservation.

We identified this as a typical donor-NGO-community liaison. Just as with wildlife conservation, the problem was identified as people, and conservation of the violet became an either-or paradigm. Reviving the people's centuries-old symbiotic relationship with the forest (which has only recently come under strain from a growing population and land hunger) was apparently considered unrealistic. Instead, says "Saving the Species," a posting on the website Rob's Violets (now The Violet Barn): "The long-term goal is to maintain forests outside the Mbololo Forest so people will not need to go into this forest for their livelihood and in doing so impact the African violet habitats."

We realized that ordinary folks in Taita do not have a clue and would be astounded were they to learn that people in the US, Japan, Russia, the Scandinavian countries, and elsewhere around

Europe have formed African violet societies and clubs that profit millions of dollars from growing and displaying these flowers.

"There is at least a $50 million-a-year industry built around the interest in this flower," said Gerard Hertel, a professor of Forest Ecology and Entomology with the Department of Biology at West Chester University in Pennsylvania. Together with Kamau Wakanene Mbuthia, who in the early 2000s was working with the National Museums of Kenya, Hertel was involved in studying the violets under a project funded by the African Violet Society of America Inc. Mbuthia and Benny Bytebier of the National Museums' Taita Biodiversity Project went on to document eight separate populations of the *Saintpaulia* species in Mbololo Forest.

Upon probing, Hertel conceded that the international trade in violets has been exploitative. "To date, little has been returned to the people who depend on the habitats where the violet grows [naturally]." On their part, conservationists have been campaigning to get the local people to preserve "the necessary genetic stocks" of the violet lest they disappear. But Hertel also found cause to say that because East Africa's wild population of violets "is too small; little cash can be made in the short or long-term from harvesting them locally."

Hertel has not been alone in advancing this argument. The East African Wildlife Society (EAWLS) also engaged in a project that offered the Taita people what then the EAWLS's Director of Programmes Hadley Becha termed *innovative and alternative livelihoods*. In other words, get the Taita out of the forest. However, Becha admitted that the violets can generate income for the local people. "I am positive that the flower has an economic value." He added that the Taita have not been cultivating it because they are yet to realise this value. But why has the EAWLS not assisted them to realise this potential? "As a membership organisation, we in EAWLS can only highlight the bio-prospecting potential in the flower with the hope that our partners can take it up," Becha said. "A fundraising venture was also started with a dispatch from the Biology Department at West Chester University requesting for funds for fuel-efficient stoves, to provide technical assistance to maintain agricultural production, to help develop tree nurseries, to pay people to help plant and restore the forests that have already been removed." Potential donors were asked to direct "tax-deductible donations through the WILD Foundation of [the] US" and to "contribute a small percentage of the sales of domesticated violets to the conservation of [the] African violet."

Other methods used to raise money for the project were adding small amounts to the costs of African violets and violet-related products for conservation purposes, asking those who place orders for the flower to contribute to conservation, and asking elected representatives in Washington to increase the funding for the USAID Offices in Kenya and Tanzania to assist in violet habitat protection. Nowhere does the EAWLS mention that the Taita people, with a little imagination, the right international connections, and some capital, could cultivate the flower commercially and generate substantial cash to contribute to its conservation in more concrete terms.

The story of the African violet is a pointer to the sheer economic potential poor African countries fail to realise by listening to NGOs, whose main interest has been to redirect local people's attention to issues of little significance as foreigners go on to develop commercial products out of the biological resources found in the continent. In East Africa, this potential stretches from the marshy terrain at the coast, through the grassy savannah plains, and onto the highlands and most of the inland lakes. The region teems with a huge variety of plants, larger and lesser animals, birds, fish, and a huge population of harmful and benign insects. There are nestles, thistles, thorns, and marigolds; woodpeckers, lions, ostriches, and beetles.

Though much of this diversity is represented evenly throughout most of the region, it is in such rainforests as Kakamega in Kenya and Budongo in Uganda—which are thought to have been part of the Guineo-Congolian Rainforest that originally stretched across the continent from Guinea to Kenya—

and in the Eastern Arc Mountains and coastal forests of Kenya and Tanzania that the diversity is best demonstrated. East Africa holds one of twenty-five biodiversity hotspots in the world. Covering a mere 1.4 percent of the world's surface area, these hotspots contain 44 percent of all plant species and have larger numbers of endemic species per hectare than any other place in the world. Being part of the tropics, East Africa hosts 50 percent of the earth's biological species and 80 percent of its arthropods. Indeed, the Conservation International website says:

> The Eastern Arc Mountains and Coastal Forests hotspot stretches along most of the eastern coast of Tanzania and into extreme southeastern Kenya. The hotspot extends more than 400 kilometers inland across Tanzania towards Lake Nyasa. It also includes the offshore islands of Pemba, Zanzibar, and Mafia. A chain of upland and coastal forests, this hotspot comprises only 0.1 percent of tropical Africa's land area, yet it contains a startling 13 percent of the entire continent's vascular plants. Nine endemic primate species, like the critically endangered Tana River red colobus monkey, and the delicate African violets are among the region's best known species.

But for all this natural wealth, poverty and all its manifestations continue to grip East Africa, where the majority of people live on the margins of life. The question often asked is why the West, which can never hope to have as much natural wealth as East Africa, is able to exploit so much of the region's resources for its own benefit? More often than not, the region's low technological development is blamed for the inability of the people to fully engage in bioprospecting. Part of this explanation centres on the cultures of the region's peoples, part on the economic model applied by different countries, part on lack of capital, and part on Africa's socio-economic relationship with the rest of the world. However, few are wont to admit that Africans have allowed themselves to be swayed, if not misled, by NGOs and the global environmentalist lobby that emphasizes and funds the preservation of species at the expense of utilising such species to meet the growing needs of local communities.

The irony is that even as environmentalists beat their conservation drums, various private Western interests are engaged in a long-running, thinly veiled plunder of Africa's biodiversity resources. For instance, in Madagascar, two anticancer drugs— vinblastine and vincristine—were made from the Madagascar periwinkle (*Catharanthus roseus*) by the pharmaceutical firm the Eli Lily Company. Though the two drugs are said to generate $100 million per year for the company, none of this is shared with Madagascar.

In Kenya, many native communities in the highlands discovered and have used *Prunus africana* to treat what they called "the old-man's disease" or swelling of the prostate glands. But they had yet to master how to exploit it on a commercial scale. This was until Jonathan Leakey, the older brother of Richard Leakey, came along.

Endemic to the highlands of Cameroon, the Democratic Republic of Congo, Equatorial Guinea, Kenya, Tanzania, and Uganda, *Prunus africana* is a slow-growing indigenous tree species whose healing properties are said to have been discovered in South Africa about 400 years ago. Modern scientific research has established that pygeum powder, which is extracted from the bark of the tree, provides relief from prostatic hyperplasia, a swelling of the prostate gland, and prevents the development of prostate cancer.

Following this, a lucrative trade in its bark emerged, with the World Agro-Forestry Centre (ICRAF) revealing that a kilogram of powdered extract was retailing at about $12,000 on the international market. Indeed, in early 2002, CNN reported that the international trade in prunus bark was worth $220 million a year. But, according to experts at the ICRAF, only a negligible proportion of this vast fortune ever trickled down to the true owners of the tree.

In Kenya, Jonathan Leakey was licensed by the KWS's Convention for International Trade in Endangered Species (CITES) office to export the prunus bark in the early 1990s when his brother, Richard, was at the helm. But in 2003, a local group led by Eustace Gitonga, who then headed the Community Museums of Kenya (CMK), took Jonathan Leakey to the National Environment Management Authority over what CMK programme officer Issa Mohamed termed *massive deprunisation* of the forest of Tugen Hills. This is a 100-kilometer stretch of indigenous forest on the western escarpment of the Rift Valley.

During the NEMA proceedings, Leakey denied that he had been harvesting the bark from government protected forests as alleged by the CMK and said he had instead been buying the bark from local farmers. A former environment minister, the late Newton Kulundu, later cancelled Leakey's export permit despite the latter's plea to be allowed to export a 25-tonne consignment of the bark he had retained from earlier extraction. *The Economist* reported in late 2003 that the trade in prunus bark rose from 200 tons in 1980 to about 3,500 tons, 68 percent going to the German market where Leakey was the main supplier to the pharmaceutical company Bayer.

Bioprospecting is big business in the US, Europe, China, and most other developed countries. Scientists at the Nairobi-based International Centre for Insect Physiology and Ecology (ICIPE) estimate per year naturally derived medicine generates over $400 billion, agrochemicals generate $30 billion, and commercial seeds generate $30 billion, while industrial enzymes generate over $1.5 billion. In addition, the World Health Organization (WHO) estimates that herbal medicinal products, food supplements, flavours, and fragrances add $60 million to the wealth already wielded by citizens of developed countries. Bioprospecting potential is even greater when it comes to insects.

But as a former head of the Bioprospecting Programme at the ICIPE, Wilber Luande, says, Africa—where 80 percent of the population relies on traditional medicine—does not feature anywhere in the list of the top earners from bioprospecting. Instead of fighting for their share, top officials of African countries prefer to plead with the European Union, the US, and other developed countries to be allowed to sell their biological resources at a pittance. Such resources often undergo only minor modifications before being resold to Africans for a fortune.

For its part, the shaky private sector in Africa has largely opted out of bioprospecting, thus failing to capitalise on emerging opportunities from biological resources. And to make matters worse, NGOs have been deployed to secure local communities' goodwill so that an exclusive group of very rich, white Kenyans and foreign profiteers can continue enjoying the resources taken from the country initially through lopsided colonial treaties, such as the Anglo-Maasai treaties of the early 1900s, or through a well-crafted grand manipulation.

NGOs have also been working for the maintenance of a status quo that shuns the majority and keeps the minority swimming in riches and untold luxury. And, as the authors came gradually to understand through our different experiences and lines of work, challenging the status quo by demanding a return of the local people's ancestral land and other resources can result in grave consequence on those who dare—as it happened to a young Maasai lawyer in early 2005.

Elijah Marima Sempeta's struggles to correct historical injustices related to land ownership may have resulted in his death, which has not been explained to date. Several months before he was murdered, the tall, light-skinned man had scoured archives in London for documents the Maasai would need to file a suit against both the British and Kenyan governments over the community's land losses in the early 1900s.

On many occasions, Sempeta had publicly questioned why the Magadi Soda Company (now owned by Tata Chemicals of India) had continued to monopolise the exploitation of soda ash in Lake Magadi. The suave and polished lawyer would find himself exhibiting visible anger as he described how the 222,788 acres the

Magadi Soda Company now sits on was excised from what was
formerly Maasai land. To back up his case, he secured copies of a
ninety-nine-year lease given to the company on November 1, 1924,
by then Governor and Commander-in-Chief of the Colony and
Protectorate of Kenya Edward William Macleay Grigg.

The documents pointed out that the lease could be extended
up to 2023 and that for the company to continue exploiting the
resource, all it needed to do was to pay an annual rent of twenty
Kenyan shillings ($0.228). After knowing this, Sempeta could not
bring himself to accept how a company that was then reputed to be
the largest producer of soda ash in Africa had been paying so little
for more than eighty years. After interviewing Sempeta, Mbaria
needed to hear the other side of the story. So, in February 2004, he
travelled to Magadi and met then Chief Executive at Magadi Soda
James Mathenge who, in defense, said that besides the rent, the
company was also paying millions of shillings in royalties to the
Kenyan government and hundreds of thousands more to the
Olkejuado County Council as rates.

But Sempeta was not convinced. He was to engage in a series
of daring acts. At one point, he even registered a company, Maa
Resources, with the intention of exploiting soda ash from Lake
Magadi for possible industrial use by the Maasai community. And
before engaging in this activism, the soft-spoken, eloquent, but
sharp-tongued lawyer had also argued—in the full glare of local
media—that the 1904 Anglo-Maasai Agreement had expired (in
2004) and the time had come for remnants of the colonial order to
return the lands they still occupy (many of which now constitute
wildlife conservancies) in Laikipia, Nakuru, and elsewhere to the
Maasai. But this was to remain a dream. Sempeta was killed on
March 9, 2005, near his home in Ngong Town, twenty-seven
kilometres southwest of Nairobi.

Sempeta's arguments were in sync with Lotte Hughes who in
Moving the Maasai: A Colonial Misadventure says that the land
occupied by the Maasai before the onset of British colonial rule
stretched from Mount Kilimanjaro right across the then Anglo-

German boundary (now the Kenya-Tanzanian border) to Laikipia and Baringo in the north. Inhabiting such vast territory, communities were able to fashion their livestock economy around rational grazing. This entailed migrating with their herds in tandem with changes in climatic conditions in such a way that they would be in the low lands during wet seasons and move to higher grounds in times of drought.

A big chunk of these lands are now under wildlife protected areas or community conservation schemes that were started at the behest of and bankrolled by NGOs led by the Northern Rangelands Trust (NRT). Their blueprint has been to secure as much land as possible under the guise of wildlife conservation. And, as we show in subsequent chapters, they have succeeded to a great extent, now able to boast control of 33,000 square kilometers of Kenyan real estate, ranging from the Laikipia and Samburu areas to northeastern areas of Ijara in Garissa County, as well as parts of Lamu County on the Kenyan Coast.

To ensure such lands are preserved for ages to come, the NGOs have been working hard to get Kenya to unwittingly forfeit and therefore forget ever accessing such lands for any sort of infrastructure development. Among the methods used has been to get the United Nations Educational, Scientific, and Cultural Organization (UNESCO) to declare such areas as World Heritage sites. But what often escapes public attention is that some of the places that the NRT has been securing share the same rock formations with areas where oil, coal, natural gas, and other minerals have been discovered in Kenya. The fact that this has been happening in a country that is yet to comprehensively map out its mineral potential means the conservation NGOs have managed, through agreements with unwitting community groups, to put under their control much of the lands suspected to hold Kenya's mineral wealth.

Once this was done, the course of action NGOs have now taken has been to use their influence in government circles and with Kenyan legislators to get them to enact laws that ensure such lands are protected. This has been going on at a time when the world's attention is gripped on Africa as the last frontier for resources, and the role that NGOs have taken has created a dangerous precedent.

Initially, it was only private companies that were involved in massive landgrabs in such countries like Mali, Malawi, Tanzania, and Kenya. But it is now clear that conservation NGOs have been facilitating a different form of landgrab in which local people are led to falsely believe that they stand to gain by setting up wildlife conservancies through a grand conservation scheme that has no parallels. Working in this scheme in Kenya are NGOs like the Northern Rangelands Trust, The Nature Conservancy, Laikipia Wildlife Forum, and the Kenya Land Conservation Trust.

Another NGO that stands out in this scheme is The Nature Conservancy, which is partially funded by the US Congress and private multinational companies. It states as its mission that it is about conserving the lands and waters on which all life depends. TNC goes on to say that it has been "working with you to make a lasting difference around the world in more than thirty-five countries, all fifty states, and your backyard."

Among the African countries, TNC has a presence in Kenya, Tanzania, Zambia, Namibia, Gabon, and the West Indian Ocean. It has found a niche in operating in the remote corners of beneficiary countries. Usually, these are places with little or no development or progress as defined by the philosophical perspectives and socioeconomic value systems handed over to Africa by the West. It says that its vision for Africa is rooted in the people who own much of the continent's lands and waters communally but "have not always been at the table during planning for a sustainable future."

To fill, this gap, TNC says it has been involving the occupants of the lands, and particularly indigenous folks, in protecting shared resources. For example, it has joined with USAID and the UK Department for International Development (DFID) to fund the Northern Rangelands Trust, which in 2014 had an annual budget of $23,529,412 and had gone public on how it has managed to bring into its fold thirty-three community conservancies that cover 44,000 square kilometers (over ten million acres). To put this figure into perspective, it covers over 7 percent of Kenya's entire land mass of 582,650 square kilometers.

The NRT has stated, "Together with dedicated conservation partners, national governments, and with your support, we aim to protect over ten million acres of private and communal lands in northern Kenya." And as the NRT does so, it has managed to keep the Kenyan government out of the picture, which in itself raises suspicion on the true purpose of securing such lands. It has nevertheless secured overwhelming support from big-time game ranchers whose sprawling properties happen to be adjacent to these community lands.

Most of these ranchers live in a near-exclusive area in eastern and parts of northern Kenya. Initially, most operated as purely private profit-making entities but have now been converting themselves into nonprofit organizations. Publicly, they say that doing so helps them to work closely with adjacent communities in saving wildlife from poachers, avoiding habitat loss, and tackling runaway insecurity. But they also operate exclusive, high-end tourist facilities that can only be described as Kenya's version of natural paradises stashed away from the toil and moil of local people and the debilitating poverty prevalent in many parts of the country.

For instance, within the Lewa Wildlife Conservancy are the Lewa Safari Camp (for twenty-four guests), Lewa House (for twelve guests), and a sixteen-guest camping facility operated by Ambercrombie and Kent. Management uses flowery language to entice and capture the imagination of tourists:

> Large tented bedrooms with verandahs and full en suite bathrooms, Lewa Safari camp offers authentic comfort for its visitors; cozy log fires in the sitting room are perfect for relaxing after a day in the Conservancy. This unique and exclusive retreat

offers privileged access to 65,000 acres of private protected wilderness. If you would like to experience the unique atmosphere and incredible setting of Lewa Safari Camp, get in touch with us today to discuss the requirements for your bespoke safari.

Ian Craig has been the ever-present face behind the world famous Lewa Wildlife Conservancy, an over-protected 62,000-acre piece of Kenya's wilderness perched at the foothills of Mount Kenya, in which Britain's royal son William toured to propose to Kate Middleton in 2010. The management complements the conservancy's international fame with occasional promotional expeditions to the US and different parts of Europe.

Like most tourist facilities in Kenya, Lewa's facilities were built with American and European clients in mind, and others who can afford the otherwise prohibitive cost of spending a night there. At $738.67 a night (the cost might be lower or higher depending on the season), this—together with a grant from the Ford Foundation—has meant Lewa was able to raise its revenue from $174,019 in 1998/99 to $304,919 in 2001/02. And also due to its fame, as a World Bank Project Status Report narrated, Lewa has been booking 100 percent occupancy during the high-tourism season and 60 percent in the low season. But even with such high income, the Craig-led management, has found it in order to raise cash from donors.

The private outfit has continued to raise donations under the guise of financing the security of wildlife and community conservation schemes, and educating local people about the value of and need to conserve the wildlife and their habitats. But this last is contested by many indigenous Kenyans who find it patronizing, obnoxious, and annoying. Indeed, some say that if there is anyone who requires such education, it is Africans of European descent and certain of their cousins in Europe and America, particularly those who find no qualms as they pay top dollar to finish off what remains of the once vast number of African species through pleasure hunts.

However, even the people who claim this miss part of the argument. Lewa and other ranches have been raising cash to bribe local people with water projects, cattle dips, and other forms of community support because the owners are aware that although they have been taking the lion's share of the proceeds from wildlife-based tourism, they do not have more rights to such proceeds than the people whose ancestral lands that now constitute the ranches were forcefully taken by colonial authorities and whose traditional conservation ethics are responsible for what remains of Kenya's wildlife resources. But long years of tokenism, piloting, bribes to leaders, and open placating of the local people through NGOs has so far ensured that those enjoying the biggest slice of the conservation cake avoid riots or other ugly scenarios that could jeopardize the flow of dollars.

For Lewa, the evocation of the needs of local people in its fund-raising campaign has paid off very handsomely over the years. But as they offer grants to this and other nonprofit outfits set up by commercial companies, the grant givers are well aware of the deception. For instance, officials of such public-funded entities as the Global Environment Facility (GEF) were fully aware that they were funding a private, profit-making entity when, in the early 2000s, they pumped into Lewa a Grant of $3.943 million for a project that the GEF went onto describe as one that "supports and further develops the activities of a private Kenyan wildlife conservation company."

And with such generous funding, big-time private game ranchers have gone ahead to establish their own conservation militias. Composed mainly of local herdsmen, the militias are trained by private security companies, some of which are owned by kin and kith of the ranch owners. These include 51 Degrees Ltd., a company associated with Batian Craig, the son of Ian Craig, who was born and raised in Lewa, educated at the exclusive Pembroke

House School near Gilgil Town, and is now a security and operations advisor.

Such companies train herders on gun handing, field operations, and typical operations in war scenarios. Once they are trained, Craig and other white game ranchers go on to secure firearms licenses and police reservist status for the trainees. But reports have it that some of the ranchers do not treat the trained guards well. Most of the militiamen are former herdsmen and *askaris* and are routinely treated with disdain by their land-owner bosses. Their training enables them as tactically skilled operatives, but because some bosses still treat them rudely, patronizingly, and occasionally with open racism, this has been a recipe for disaster. For instance, in 2013 Ol Jogi Conservancy fired twenty-two of twenty-five trained personnel and has reaped the bitter fruits of rampant poaching since then. Other heavily guarded conservancies like Ol Pejeta, Lewa, and Solio have suffered similar difficulties.

But this is not all. A number of ranches own unregistered airstrips, and some have used NGOs to request the US government for sophisticated surveillance equipment, including drones. The move to acquire the drones (or "air rangers") became public on May 24, 2012, when Iain Douglas-Hamilton, the Founder of the Save the Elephants NGO, was invited to give testimony on poaching in Africa by the US Senate Committee on Foreign Affairs.

In his talk, "Ivory and Insecurity: The Global Implication of Poaching in Africa," Douglas-Hamilton pleaded with America to donate helicopters, planes, remote sensors, and gunshot indicators, as well as drones, for the antipoaching war in Africa. This plea was accentuated in 2013 when the Ol Pejeta Wildlife Conservancy teamed up with the California-based firm Airware to build and test drones in the conservancy. Each drone had the capability of covering some eighty kilometres besides being able to fly for more than one and a half hours nonstop. They were also fitted with a live streaming HD camera with 360 degree remote controlled viewing and GPS to store images and give location coordinates. Apart from surveillance, the company had also planned to use the drones to launch the first virtual tourism village in Kenya, with the aim of broadcasting it to tourists in real time.

But the scheme for a full-scale drone launch was nixed by the Kenyan government at the end of May 2014 over security concerns. Revealing this to the media, the conservancy's chief commercial officer, Robert Breare, and public relations manager, Elodie Sampere, said in a joint statement, "The Kenyan government has put a ban on private sector drones for the time being." The story attracted significant public interest when it was published by Kenya's biggest newspaper, the *Daily Nation* on May 30, 2014, and there was widespread reaction from Kenyans, with over 123 readers posting comments online—many of whom expended a generous helping of adjectives to lambast the government for not being serious about the antipoaching war. Some, though, expressed suspicion over why a foreign-owned game ranch would want to operate such sophisticated surveillance equipment in an area close to Kenyan and British military installments. "The drone issue is just a disguise, especially with the British Army operating in Northern Kenya and based in Nanyuki. We need to be wary of who we allow to manage our skies," lamented one reader. Another said, "Ol Pejeta is near our military base in Nanyuki. We don't want Americans snooping on it."

Much can be said and asked about the efficacy (or lack thereof) of employing drones as a conservation tool. However, any observant person who has toured Ol Pejeta will tell you that for an outsider to penetrate the fences, find an elephant or rhino, shoot it, and make a clandestine exit is close to impossible. The security there is too tight. Such an event would most likely be an inside job, so this would be the resolute application of an engineering solution to a human problem.

As stated here, many also speculate about possible ulterior security motives of having these drones near military installations. The truth is probably more mundane; it's more likely to be the number of highly paid jobs, donor funds, and PR mileage to be gained by having unmanned aerial vehicles monitoring critically endangered species out in the jungles of Africa. The practiced (and jaded) observer's eye can scent millions of dollars in donor and research funding, virtual tourism, and even movie rights. The one thing, though, that is difficult to see potentially accruing from this project is a sustainable conservation of African wildlife and its habitats.

3 ~ Role of African Culture in Conservation: Talk is Cheap

The oppressive community conservation myth: The exogenous tourism model relentlessly sells a product that expressly excludes Samburu pastoralists and their livestock from vast tracts of their own land. (©Mordecai Ogada)

The Hamlet

Once upon a hamlet, there lived a people. Their homes, worship, and ceremonies were far removed from the world as known then. They lived large. But that was during a different time and different circumstances. Most did not know what it meant to go without food or the other essentials of life. Still, they thankfully looked up to their gods in reverence, praying for their needs and performing rituals to clean up their misdeeds.

 And in the darkest of nights, they lit torches, blew gushes of air to keep fires alive, and danced vigorously under the dim moonlight. And as nights wore on, many smeared the darkness with love and sweat, siring hefty babies at day break. The hamlet thanked its gods for the rain, beseeching them to keep sickness at bay and the land awash with abundance.

Thousands of moons came and went; the people slumbered. Most took for granted what the gods had abundantly provided. Then, strangers happened to the hamlet. The new men and their women were indeed peculiar: they could remove their legs, could hang their eyes on the wall, and travel while seated. And wearing long robes and longer faces, their priests sung sad hymns to a god born in lands afar.

And in sheer audacity, the strange priests told the hamlet's people that their gods were no more. At first, the people could not believe this. Didn't our gods bless the land with waterfalls, trees, sunshine, beetles, and elephants? The hamlet people sat for long hours in the village square wondering what might have gotten into the heads of the strange priests.

Somehow, a number of the hamlet people kept listening to the awkward story. Some took the strange priests' words as truth. But most in the hamlet kept older beliefs. All, including the king and his court, believed the strangers were only on some sojourn from other lands far away from the hamlet. Strangers, they reasoned, are like river water: they are here today, somewhere else tomorrow. Once they were done with their incessant wandering, the people believed the strangers would go home and leave the hamlet to its devises.

But the strangers went nowhere. Soon, they put up a fort on which they hoisted a multicoloured piece of clothing they called a flag. The strange priests, the Hamlet observed, were accompanied by soldiers with pipes that smoked death on to anyone who resisted as their land and cattle were taken away. On their part, the strange priests constructed their own shrines near the sacred tree. And with sugar, cowry, cotton, and copious narratives of a son of god gifted with the power to heal, feed, and feel everyone's pain, some of the hamlet's scions agreed to sing the new songs to the new deity. Most pitied the godman who, they were told, had died up on a tree after been molested for long hours by evil soldiers. As they prayed for long and sung hard, the kind hamlet people were forgiven new sins that they had not committed. And when they were showered with small gifts of sugar, old khaki shorts, and strange mannerisms, the new people started looking at their ancestors' ways with disdain. What, they asked, did our forefathers ever make? Akala for shoes?

To this new people, the ancient shrines were no longer sacred. The spirits of trees and animals and brooks no longer mattered; such spirits could as well jump into River Kathita—who cared! The hamlet dances changed.

Circumcision songs became too obscene. It was no longer fashionable to do the harvest jig in the square. The sacred river where age-old rites were performed became just a river. The people could no longer offer sacrifices to gods—the godman and his father demanded no sacrifices; he had made the last sacrifice. Natural shrines were no longer necessary; the people could build a home for the godman. With prompting from the new priests, the people reasoned that the godman had indeed freed everyone from the eternal fear of sacred trees, graveyards, witchcraft, and spirits of the dead. Didn't our new priests say that we do not belong to this world?

As the strangers continued to plant their flag everywhere on the land and as he ruled over men and women, the hamlet aided him to soil everything. Soon, the hamlet had millions of tree stumps, filthy streams, unmarried mothers, uncared-for orphans, gonorrhea, education . . . and progress! Long years passed and pestilence, genocidal wars, and conflicts visited the hamlet with deaths and misery unseen before. The rains still came, but failed when needed or came at the wrong time or in torrents that washed away the hamlet's fertile soils. Granaries were no longer built because there were no harvests to keep because the soils could no longer accept to be bribed with chemicals made by the strangers. Many rivers ceased to flow. Deep craters remained wherever the strangers and their local hands disemboweled the earth in search of gold, copper, and tin.

Soon, a people forgot to love, swapped crime for friendship and money for brotherhood . . . as sex became the new religion.

After several generations, the strangers retreated. Some went back to die in the lands of their fathers. A few forfeited their right to be buried next to their ancestors and made the hamlet their permanent home. But those who remained were not happy with the progress the hamlet's people had made. Didn't we teach these people gentler jigs? Didn't we arm them with polished manners? Was it not us that gave the hamlet the right to light? Why can't they be like us? they wondered.

But the hamlet's people had indeed learned much more than the strangers could bring themselves to accept. They had grown the hamlet into a city where people nurtured not crops nor flocks but jealousy, crime, greed, deceit . . . more education, more development. Soon, there was hardly enough to satiate unfettered greed. The people had now permanently lost their soul; the spirit that held the hamlet together was no more. They had also lost their right to think. The strangers' ways occupied their inner longings. Those able pushed, shoved, robbed, and killed to sit on the seats and to eat at the tables the strangers had left behind, occupying, as they said, the right side of history. The godman now rode roughshod over age-old gods and enjoyed incessant worship by millions in the strangers' shrines. A select few thanked the godman for making it possible to eat more than their fill and to throw away whatever they could not eat or keep. But these were crafty men who courted craftier women; men who gained access to the high table ensured that those who could not join them in eating forever begged them to continue eating on their behalves.

So, no one questioned the stranger's ways. Decenters risked the wrath of the entire city if they entertained older thoughts or worshipped the gods of their fathers and their fathers' fathers. They had to sing in harmony with everyone else. They had to bellow praises to the strangers, even when the strangers took to the bush to shoot buffaloes for fun, while it meant death if the hamlet people were to take to the woods in search of a dik-dik for mboga. The stranger had, by then, made the land awash with guns, his own laws, and money, while swift men were trained to keep vigil and to spit death unto those who went against the grain.

And the hamlet was now civilized. No one worried about taboos. Most mocked the spirits of trees and beetles while others cursed the rain and unwanted foetuses landed in pits full of human dung. Emblems of older gods were defaced. Everyone could now travel while seated and buy love and happiness in shops. Some found themselves falling sick and dying from eating too much. Others were equally free to eat nothing and be outwardly happy about it. Nobody bothered as naughty, shameless boys and girls defecated in the river. After all, giant machines had done more than their part in defacing the whole place, spitting torrents of urine and unsightly dung into streams and rivers where new initiates once bathed. What was more, anyone with money could summon the law to protect them as they drained all manner of dirt into those streams and rivers as well. Powerful and moneyed men and their womenfolk could now kill millions of trees for profit, deny the hyena its home, and be decorated as Elders of the Burning Forest during national celebrations.

As the hamlet allowed itself to be destroyed, its people believed that the gods that had kept them in natural bondage were no more; their place had been taken forever by the gods of silver and gold, roads, concrete, money, stocks, foreign assistance, and sex.

And as the hamlet died, the strangers continued to demand that its people thank them for it.

~ John Mbaria (2011)

The above narration describes, within a measure of accuracy, one of the most far-reaching and noticeable legacies of colonialism and neo-colonialism in Kenya and elsewhere in Africa. It narrates the deliberate, systematic, multipronged, and malicious destruction of the African soul, its culture, way of life, and resources. It also talks about how everything natural and organic to Africa has continued to be replaced with inappropriate and unworkable solutions, leading to situations that have created all manner of crises.

Further, it talks of a scenario in which the victims are either blamed for the crises or implored, through media and intellectual input, to remain thankful for being pushed to the edge. Whenever he is not asked to pay homage to the European mission of civilization and a development model that has destroyed much of what was good and worked for him, the African is made to keep blaming himself for the yoke placed on him by others. What is more, any attempt at ridding Africa of this yoke is thwarted by a global trade-cum-geopolitical-cum-governance order that relegates the continent to the periphery, a foreign-aid chicanery that takes much more than it gives, and an elaborate media-dominated deception that frustrates any real effort at emancipation.

Strategically positioned with funds and the wherewithal is a local ruling class that provides the muscle for the maintenance of this exploitative order while a noisy civil society keeps churning out situational reports on every aspect of the continent's peoples, which are later used to craft ever smarter schemes of maintaining the prevailing stranglehold without making the continent's people feel like they want to rise against it.

But how did Africa get into this situation?

The European colonial administrations—and particularly the British—were not content with unleashing untold violence and robbing Africans of their natural resources, sweat, and man-made wealth. From the very beginning, they made a deliberate and systematic effort to thoroughly understand—for the purpose of manipulation—the cultures and traditions of the colonized peoples. Towards this end, they unleashed anthropologists, such as Isaac Schapela, who was asked to look at the way European colonial rule could benefit from anthropology; Philip Guliver, whose anthropological training and understanding of local communities primed him for his later work as a colonial administrator; Louis Seymour Bazett Leakey (L. S. B. Leakey), who authored a most comprehensive ethnographic study of the Gikuyu people. Indeed, Kenya's first president, Jomo Kenyatta, who wrote *Facing Mount Kenya,* was a student of one of the most eminent anthropologists of the 1930s, Bronislaw Malinowsky.

These anthropologists had the support of colonial administrations, who looked forward to using their reports toward a sure footing in the continent and to craft a most effective technology for domination and control. For instance, L. S. B. Leakey, who was financially supported by the Rhodes Trust to research the customs of the Gikuyu people in 1937, says in his book *Southern Kikuyu Before 1903* that he received "every assistance" from government officials but differed "very strongly" with some who viewed his study as a purely academic undertaking. To him, the study's utility was in helping to get a grip on Gikuyu rebellion against colonial rule. He wrote; "I believe that it is impossible to study and understand the present day problems in the [G]ikuyu tribe without knowledge of what their laws and customs were before the impact of European civilization."

Unlike Leakey, who studied anthropology and archeology at the University of Cambridge, most of those who wrote on the customs and social organization of different ethnic groups in Kenya were not professional anthropologists. They were missionaries, travelers, and administrators who recorded regarding the cultures of the people they encountered or ruled. Later, the International African Institute (formerly the International Institute of African Languages and Cultures) was launched in 1926 to promote research and knowledge on African cultures and to make such knowledge available for use by the European colonial administrators, educators, and missionaries. Fredrick Lugard, the man who came up with the indirect-rule policy, was the Institute's first director. (Indirect-rule was a system of government often used by the British and French to control parts of their colonial empires, particularly in Africa and Asia, through preexisting local power structures. The dependencies thus formed were referred to as *protectorates* or *trucial states.*)

The Europeans combined such knowledge of local cultures, sheer brutality, deliberate disease epidemics, such as smallpox, sanctimonious tendencies, and enticements to subdue, pacify, and consistently rub from the natives' psyches long-held cultures and traditions. This helped the colonialists to achieve what Caroline Elkins, Professor of History and African and African American Studies at Harvard University, calls an "astonishing portrait of destruction."

Colonialists were more particular and brutally systematic with ethnic groups that dared to wage different levels of resistance to their occupation and rule. Unto such groups, the colonial administrations went out of their way to consistently and perversely rubbish what it was that held the people together or made them tick. The ironic twist in this infamy was the Europeans used different means to make the Africans feel that all this was to promote their own good. And, as Professor Elkins says, the Europeans were also infected by virulent racism:

> To the settler, there was nothing noble about the African "savage." Many believed the African to be biologically inferior, with smaller brains, a limited capacity to feel pain or emotion, and even different nutritional needs, requiring only a bowl of

maize meal, or *posho*, to maintain their health. African men had to be controlled; they were unpredictable and sexually aggressive, threatening both white women and the maintenance of their idealized chastity as well as the racial purity of the colony's European community.

The big idea here was to totally destroy Africans as they were known then and establish in them a clean slate on which Europeans could bequeath a long-lasting desire for a *better* way of life and a hankering for everything European. As colonialism took hold in the continent, and as African people's cultural structures and perceptions of themselves became so ravaged, many of the brutalized people began looking at their own ways of life with disdain. What the Europeans could not steal they destroyed.

Uncannily, and through the repetitive Goebbels approach to propaganda, many an African started believing that it was for their own benefit that what was good about them was destroyed. It then became easy for Africans to acquiesce and even to participate in throwing to the dogs what had thrived for ages. This has continued to date, with intellectuals, the media, and books being deployed as attack dogs ever ready to belittle anyone who complains of the lasting negative legacy of Europeans' forceful occupation of Africa and to redirect the blame to the Africans inability to wriggle themselves out of colonialism's most far-reaching adverse effects that continue to fester.

The long-running and systematic destruction of a sophisticated cultural way of life manifests itself best in the way the African child was and continues to be nurtured from a tender age in the four corners of the classroom. As she sits silently, as she attentively listens to the teacher, the child is somehow expected to figure out how, for instance, the very water that she drinks is made up of two parts hydrogen and one part oxygen. The child is expected to conceptualise this fascinating scientific reality through an alien language, chalk, and the teacher's accented tongue.

In the school, too, children are no longer taught through different mediums that promote local cultures, such as songs their forebears sang to glorify heroism, justice, fairness or that heap praises on big-humped Nguni cows, bountiful harvests, and beautiful birds. No longer are children given the opportunity to appreciate the life-sustaining roles played by the elements through songs, such as one in which the singer promises to slaughter copious numbers of young bulls if the rain continues showering its welcome blessings on the land. Instead, school children are taught to sing about a bridge in London that broke down, about how John the slave is to have a new master, about an elderly Father William who shamelessly stands on his head, about a mirror that glorifies Cinderella's stunning beauty, or copious songs about a godman, Jesus, on whose mercy the child survives, lives, and thrives.

Natural images are substituted for others that, for instance, depict God as white and Satan as a black, hideous fiend. In schools, children are no longer allowed to speak in their native tongues; that is a too primitive and uncivilised way of communicating. Such disdain for native tongues was evidenced in Kenya in February 2014 after the Education Ministry announced its intention to implement a policy requiring pupils in lower primary to be taught in their mother tongues. The announcement generated much more heat than light with naysayers condemning the ministry for attempting to worsen tribalism in a country so ravaged by this vice.

In Kenya, education is merely a means via which the learner is readied—through the indoctrination of Western knowledge and skills—for a competitive, capitalistic economy in which securing a job is the overriding goal. Those who craft the philosophy, mission, and vision of the education sector have never considered it a means for reestablishing the vital links between the people and the environment or the interconnectedness between humanity and everything else. And though the Kenyan government states in policy documents the importance of retaining respect for and developing African cultures as one of the national goals of education, students are never given the opportunity to learn about or reconnect with their own cultures for a thorough self-appreciation that would consequently enable them to embrace a more affirming world view, if not a more sustainable development process. Neither does education in Kenya create in students the desire to reestablish themselves as distinct human beings, capable and different in a globalised world, or the desire for true liberation.

Right from the word go, the child is denied the opportunity to learn about the history and cultures of her people. She is also denied an opportunity to learn how her people interacted with the environment and how such interaction led to the attainment of a varied hierarchy of needs and wants. This has gone on against the best wishes and intentions of pioneering history scholars, such as Prof. Bethwell A. Ogot, who not only have been keen to have history taught in schools but have also constantly voiced the view that history syllabi need to encourage critical thinking on the larger issues facing students, their country, and the world. Ogot writes, "History [has] to discourage a return to dry facts, patriotic indoctrination, and history for its own sake and instead teach the subject so that historical data [is] brought to bear directly on the larger questions facing our nation and the world, questions that [impinge] on the students' lives."

But as it turned out, Professor Ogot and company lost the argument to a fraternity of social-studies educators. Sponsored by foreign foundations, the latter would hear nothing about history being taught in primary schools. They succeeded in having history lessons removed from primary school curriculums in Kenya and a number of other African countries and replaced them with social studies. "They wanted to throw out the kind of history we were championing, convinced that in the 'global village,' there was no place to dig up the past," Ogot says. Thus, foreign aid was given to cooperating African governments, so that they could scrap history lessons in primary schools and replace them with social studies in the belief that the latter would enable learners to readily acquiesce themselves to the dictates of a globalizing, exploitative economic order.

By doing so, the British and other major powers have ensured that at her most impressionable age, the African child will never get an opportunity to appreciate her heritage—natural or manmade. The big idea here is to ensure that as she goes through school, and as she goes through life, the child is systematically alienated from her culture, history, and heritage, and that she finally forgets or, at worse, looks down on anything that ever defined her people. But even as this happens, what is intriguing is just how much the ruling and policy-making classes have been willing to be duped by moneymen from the north so as to sacrifice some of the remaining opportunities for unequivocal liberation of the continent's peoples at the altar of pitiful foreign aid.

This scenario replays itself in an uglier form in religion. The African came into contact with missionaries who, according to Professor Elkins, were determined to convert him not just to Christianity but to an entire Western way of life. The African was again and again and over long years told, through many medias, that his way of worship was not merely inferior, it was heathen, the way of the savage, and irredeemably satanic. Initially, the European missionaries did not openly antagonize the gods worshiped by Africans. They were subtle about it, making the African believe that there was only one God who was worshipped by all humanity. However, the attitude the missionaries harboured and later voiced on traditional African worship systems did not often agree with the holier-than-thou lessons they imparted to their converts. Among other things, converts were told that failing to do away with their earlier system of worship and lifestyle was a sure way of securing their place in hell after this life. And as it was described by the white missionaries, hell is not a place anybody would yearn to be—it was said to be the abode of the infinitely evil, where the supreme fiend, Lucifer, draws immense but malicious pleasure from hurling sinful people into vast, everlasting flames.

Those who failed the Christian test of righteousness or did not obey the European god were, and continue to be, promised an eternity of endless anguish. It was described as the final torment for polygamous people who, in European thinking, committed life-long adultery and who, as the new thinking in the West goes, are worse than the worst violators of human rights and dignity. God, converts were told, is infallible and omniscient and is not pleased by polygamy; he created just one wife for Adam, Eve. Anyone who committed such and other African sins was eternally damned. Hell would be the reward for people who coveted other people's wives, stole, told lies, rustled cattle, or mentioned the name of the European god in vain. Unto the African psyche was consistently drummed up more commandments than the original ten said to have been given to the Israelite patriarch Moses by the white god.

As lesson upon lesson was preached to Africans on how to live the righteous European life, they were soon made to do away with animal sacrifices. The African was also made to stop paying homage to departed spirits through repeated religious teachings that equated any reverence to them with worshipping Satan. There was no longer any differentiation—as was made in traditional African religions—between good and evil spirits. In Christianity, the spirits of the dead either take to heaven or hell; none remain on earth, so the converts needed not appease them any longer.

The missionaries also led converts in the denigration of important and revered African traditional religious symbols and concepts. For instance, they equated the Gikuyu word *icua-ini* with hell. But prior to the coming of Christianity to Gikuyuland, *icua-ini* meant the holiest, inner-most part of the furnace where fire consumed the flesh of the animals sacrificed by *matura-nguru* elders to seek God's intervention in times of crises. Soon, converts felt no need to continue regarding with reverence the natural shrines where elders had met God and pleaded on behalf of entire communities—such sites were no longer sacred or necessary. Early Gikuyu converts, for example, abandoned the belief that Ngai inhabited the apex of Mount Kenya, and Mugumo became but a mere tree, no longer holy.

As the African child became alienated from her culture, worship, and a way of life that had sustained her people for thousands of years, she was also enticed to accept a new way of life, an alien culture that was totally removed from her day-to-day experiences. While the child previously learned vital, life-long lessons from her surroundings on the farm and in the bush—how various animals (wild and domestic) behaved, the alternating dry and wet seasons, and other components of nature—her learning was now confined to the classroom. Books, written by Europeans in their own language that betrayed a different philosophical outlook on life and humanity's place in the natural order of things replaced traditions, culture, nature, and social interaction in nurturing the African child's intellectual growth.

The English-speaking teacher, the catechist, the priest, the radio, and TV took over as parents, grannies, elders, older community members, the child's peers, and the entire society took a back seat in teaching the child. Rituals that had previously inculcated irreplaceable lessons on the interrelationships of humans and nature were dropped or demonised. And as the child received such shallow education, she became fast removed from the experiences of her people and ancestors. Natural phenomena were now merely described in the classroom, not learned through personal experiences. The child became estranged to the very practices and processes that kept her people in constant supply of food, water, clothing, building materials, and other life-sustaining ecological services. What had worked for the child's ancestors and entire ethnic communities was abandoned; those practices that could not be altered were promptly changed. The spirits of water and rain and soil and forests and elephants, which were capable of playing an important part in the life of humans and to whom sacrifices were occasionally made, were replaced by the almighty European god who had given humankind (Europeans) the right to dominate everything else on earth and had put for their use nature and all its bounty.

Soon, the African child, whose forebears had learned to constantly see God in everything and had developed such fear, awe, and respect for nature, could now destroy, dominate, and disregard. Later in life, the child found no scruples as she made trees, forests, and wildlife succumb to the lethal instruments of destruction Europeans bequeathed to Africa once its children were thoroughly assimilated into the European culture and way of life. And as a sign of how warped this new thinking has become, such unfettered destruction is now universally known as *human progress* or *development.*

As an extension to this thinking, a new form of Christian behaviour and economic pursuit that is both simplistic and fatalistic—held particularly by firebrand Pentecostal Christians—emerged. To these firebrands, Jesus literary liberated humankind from everything, cultures and traditions included. This brand of Christianity regards adherence to myths and taboos, including those that have enabled humans to live and let other species live, either as atavistic or satanic. As a result, myths that enabled communities to continue enjoying environmental services no longer hold sway over individual or societal decisions and actions.

For instance, among some farming communities in Kenya, it used to be one could not just go to a forest for the purpose of clearing and replacing it with crops. These communities once believed that forests provided veritable abodes for the spirits of the dead and that trees and other inanimate objects had their own spirits that could potently destroy one's life and therefore deserved to be respected. And so, before clearing any section of forest, a farmer had to first seek the consent of the spirits. He also had to leave some trees standing as a way of preserving the dwelling place of the spirits that resided therein.

As recorded by L. S. B. Leakey, in the Gikuyu community, this entailed a detailed ritual in which the land owner called a senior council elder with whom he would cut a branch of another tree and solemnly lean it against the stem of the tree he wished to cut down the next day. He then left for the night. When he came back the following day, he brought with him honey beer and would stand at the base of the tree and address it: "*I have come to cut you down, O tree, but I am not going to destroy the whole of the spirits which are in you. See, I have prepared a new home for them and you.*" Then he would sprinkle some honey beer on the foot of the tree as an offering for the tree spirits before carrying the branch he had placed the night earlier to another tree. This was a symbolic gesture aimed at relocating the spirits. Leakey says that a more elaborate ritual involving the sacrifice of a ram was conducted if the tree was old. To a large extent, this ensured that members of the community appreciated that just as cultivation was necessary, so was conservation of a forest, or a part of it, as well as its ecological services.

Such deep appreciation is no more. Instead, most people schooled on Western education and nurtured on its mannerisms and culture are wont to associate such an approach to nature conservation as an archaic practice bordering on voodooism. Anyone advocating for maintaining such reverence for nature is often reminded that such practices are time-barred, that Africa has moved on, and that the dictates of human population increases and the integration of different ethnic groups makes cultural conservation practices untenable.

But those who say so rarely go on to associate the Western conservation model with the dismal failure to secure biological resources that are key to human survival on the continent. No one wants to associate the rise in frequency and severity of droughts, famines, and flooding, as well as local people's vulnerability to such natural catastrophes, with a failure to adhere to practices that proved appropriate and useful for ages. Instead, climate change and other natural consequences of humanity's shortsightedness have become the bogeyman for all human misdeeds and stupidity. Those harbouring such disdain for the role of African thought systems and cultural conservation ethics fail to acknowledge that it can never be too late for a people to liberate themselves.

Further, rarely are examples pointed to of countries that have large human populations who have maintained a substantial measure of their indigenous culture and, as a result, have managed to maintain the largest portions of their territory as wilderness. For instance, Japan has more than 127 million people, but it has preserved close to 70 percent of its total land area of 377,835 square kilometers as forests!

To some extent, Christian teachings do associate God with life and death situations. But by and large, God is not associated with nature. Christians do not see God as a wholesome, integrated deity whose anger over humanity's destructive and short-sighted ways is seen in floods, droughts, or pestilences. God, or nature, has become amenable to human creativity and manipulation by capital. In everyday worship, Christians rarely make a deliberate, consistent, and intricate reference to the relationship between God and biodiversity, God and the gift of life, God and good weather, God and life-nurturing brooks full of sparkling clean water, God and flourishing herds and flocks, or God and bountiful harvests on which humans feed and maintain their good health.

It is rare—extremely rare—for Christians to associate God, in their prayers and worship, with the sperms that bulls ejaculate to sire hefty calves, seed that sprouts from the ground, elephants that are endowed with such strength and long teeth, leopards given to such stealthy ways, or lions that give definition to bravery and brutal force. God, to the Christian religion, no longer requires elders to sacrifice animals so that He can put an end to droughts, floods, disease outbreaks, or other calamities. Jesus, as the thinking goes, made the ultimate sacrifice and permanently replaced the need for animal sacrifices. God now dislikes sacrifices; He dislikes tradition; He is now a modern dot-com God.

To the contrary, African traditional religious thoughts and inclinations, as the following Gikuyu traditional prayer depicts, associated God with much more.

Ngai, of the Kirinyaga (God of the white snow),
God of the Kirimaara (that of the dotted peaks),
See how I stretch my hands,
See how I invoke your name in passion,
Let the skies conceive and give birth,
May the rivers swell and the soil turn blacker,
May the granaries remain heavy,

May the children defecate, may they urinate,
Let women give birth to twins,
May the herds be escorted by calves, ewes, and rams,
Keep diseases at bay, hide our land from the bad eye, shield us from the
worldly disasters,
Suck out the pain from our blood, give us peace of health, give us prosperity,
May the ruling generation see far, may their peace staffs grip firmly, may
their hairs turn grey,
Oooh peace, Ooooh peace, Ngai, Oooh peace, Ooooh peace, Oooh peace,
Ngai, Oooh peace

In our times, God is more likened to a human being than to a
lion or a goat or a hippopotamus or a squirrel or a hurricane. He is
a God who is like man, having made humans in his own image.
The modern understanding of God has limited his abilities, and
gradually His power has been overtaken by technology, money, and
human accomplishment. Just like the heydays of colonialism when
missionaries found no irony in ganging up with the colonial
administrators, soldiers, and settlers in robbing African societies of
their lands and livestock and killing whoever resisted, the clergy
now has acquiesced itself with ongoing robbery from and
destruction of nature and differing spirits of humanity.

It is therefore no longer a surprise that the biggest Christian
denominations in Kenya, especially the Catholic Church, have
some of the greatest and most lucrative chunks of real estate in the
country, some which were acquired under dubious circumstances.
As a result, many discerning people can no longer see the harmony
between what is preached and what is practiced; it is quite
confusing.

Indeed, before the advent of the prosperity gospel, which
teaches how the attainment of material possessions is God's way of
ascertaining his favour on adherents, missionaries had crafted a way
out of such confusion by emphasizing the uselessness of earthly
belongings. For instance, in Gikuyuland, missionaries constantly
drummed into converts that *mburi, ng'ombe, na ithaka itiri na bata;*
kindu kina bata no riiri wa Jesu (i.e., sheep, land, and cattle do not

matter; what matters is the grace of Jesus). This thinking appears to have been inspired by Solomonic teaching. Solomon, as the famous Irish playwright George Bernard Shaw said in *Man and Superman*, found life, material possessions, and an exaggerated, over-used libido useless after he finally realised that nature would not dance to his wishes.

But as the missionaries taught this antimaterialism, they continued to accumulate the same wealth they discouraged converts from acquiring. This was not the only way the missionaries continued to twist the message in the Good Book to suit a colonial agenda. Lessons were taught (and continue to be taught) that whoever has little, even whatever they have will be taken away and given to those who have more. Colonialism, just like slavery before, was justified in the name of Christianity. The missionaries did not see any contradiction between the gospel lessons they gave to the natives and the taking away of Africans' lands. Most said nothing as their settler kin utterly destroyed wildlife through hunting parties or as they cleared vast tracts of forests to pave way for a destructive and manipulative order colonial. The missionaries appeared to acquiesce even after this led to an existential threat to the Africans or when the shrines where the Africans had previously worshipped became private property, dislodging God and the spirits.

Thus schooled, African converts began seeing God as a being that lived in a church and to whom one could genuflect on Sunday or Sabbath day as they continued in their wayward ways over the rest of the week. It is no wonder that colonialism bequeathed unto Africa deceit, arrogance (against other species and within the species), and hypocrisy, which are now some of the inevitable marks of human-nature and intra-human relationships. Hypocrisy, as the former Tanzanian president the late Julius Kambarage Nyerere observed in 1952, has remained one of the most enduring legacies of European colonial rule:

There is much hypocrisy in East Africa today. The European official and the European settler rule and maintain their prestige mainly by hypocrisy, their inner motives would hardly stand examination; the Indian trader makes his living by downright dishonesty, or at best, by sheer cunning, which is hypocrisy; the African clerk or labourer often disregards fulfilling his part of a contract, and even a very educated African will pretend to love the European whereas his heart is nearly bursting with envy and hatred.

From the master twisters of the scriptures, it became possible for humans to mould God in their own image. Like their white counterpart who killed wildlife for sport and who decimated resisting communities with abandon, Africans discovered a God that could be swayed to understand and forgive them whenever they killed other life forms, degraded nature, and desecrated sacred sites. Even if He didn't understand, what could He do? By the time the colonial machinery was firmly in place, Christianity had destroyed, to a great degree, the age-old philosophy and practice that many communities had relied on to preserve the greatest diversity of life on earth. But as a mark of irretrievable arrogance and myopic understanding of human-nature relationships on the continent, some scholars in the West have claimed that the African was a victim of abundance who contributed nothing to conserve what nature so endowed him with.

But the role played by Africans in conserving nature, and particularly wildlife and forests, is not debatable. There is ample evidence that the people the West strove to categorise uncivilised did actually go out of their way to deliberately conserve nature through a variety of means. For the African, preserving nature was not something done to capture the attention of others; it was a day-to-day practice enshrined in the cultural and economic system and organically developed through the ages. It had nothing to do with any fascination cultivated among Victorian and post-Victorian Englishmen—who only developed an exaggerated, romantic affinity for nature after their widespread and systematic looting and plundering secured for them a massive rise in material wealth. As an illustration of the fact that Africans did involve themselves in deliberate conservation of nature, L. S. B. Leakey says:

> Owners of land had the absolute right to prohibit all felling of trees in certain areas, either for fuel or for any other purpose. This was in order to create timber reserves, which could be used at a later date when the forest had been pushed further back in the course of clearing for cultivation . . . an estate owner also had the right to maintain a patch of dense forest all around the area chosen for an ordinary village (*itúúra*) well inside [G]ikuyu country, as well as one chosen for the building of a fortified village.

More importantly, Leakey says that Gikuyu landowners, for instance, used curses to ensure that some of the forests that are so valued today in Nairobi City were preserved:

> A man who had bought a large area of forest sometimes left a deathbed curse prohibiting any of his descendants from ever bringing tenants on to the estate. This meant, of course, that much of the forest land could be left undisturbed.

Some of the Kenyan forests which Leakey says had "definite curses" before 1900 include the 1,063-hectare Karura Forest Reserve and the 60-hectare City Park. Karura Forest owes its very preservation to four land owners, Tharuga, Gacii, Wang'endo and Hinga, while credit for the preservation of the City Park goes to a man by the name of Kirongo, who "by his own wish, was buried there when he died." Today, these two forest reserves are considered among the most important lungs for a highly polluted Nairobi County. But again, self-acclaimed environmental do-gooders, together with the Kenya Forest Service, have never made any attempt to inform donors or Nairobi residents of the important role played by traditional African conservation ethics and cultural selflessness in preserving two of Nairobi's most important green spaces.

Instead, certain exotic conservationists and their well-to-do Kenyan counterparts have established outfits going by the names Friends of Karura Forest Community Association and Friends of Nairobi City Park, which they use for elaborate fund-raising exercises that generate millions of shillings each year from such bodies as the Africa Fund for Endangered Wildlife, Alliance Media & Ovidian, APA Insurance, Barclays Bank of Kenya Ltd., Bins Nairobi Services Ltd., Davis & Shirtliff Ltd., Cama Trading Inc., East African Breweries Ltd., G4S Security Services (Kenya) Ltd., Prime Bank Ltd., The George Drew Estate, the British Army Training Unit in Kenya (BATUK), the Federal Republic of Germany, and others. Long before they were declared by the British colonial administration and the National Museums of Kenya as nationally important assets, these areas were saved by unsung indigenous conservationists. However, copious documents are produced that continue associating the existence of Karura and Nairobi City Park with a conservation model that is largely about money, consumerism, destruction, and domination.

This is a model that has been embraced in Kenya and other African countries not by choice but through coercion and trickery. According to Dr. John Waithaka, a Canada-based conservation biologist and former KWS assistant director, the traditional resource management systems described above remained strong until 1895 when Kenya became a British protectorate and later a colony. The importance of traditional conservation ethics declined very rapidly thereafter, and they have faded into insignificance in many Kenyan communities. Dr. Waithaka attributes the attitudes currently adopted by many Kenyans on wildlife to the British style of governance and their approach to land acquisition, ownership, use, and management. Further, he says the British patterns of wildlife conservation and utilization, their establishment of protected areas, their relationship with the native people and attitudes towards African cultures, and their approach to law enforcement and responses to resistance by discontented communities all played a crucial role in shaping the ambivalent attitude harboured by many Kenyans today towards wildlife and continue to have bearing on how conservation issues are perceived and tackled.

In instances where native Africans are associated with conservation, it is merely through empty rhetoric and lip homage to conservation ethics that are not as self-serving as the model developed in the West. Many reports have lingering narrations on how different African communities spared the wildlife that others have either been killing for fun or profiting from through elaborate tourism machinery. By extension, those who write the reports go on to argue that local communities ought to share in the benefits emanating from wildlife conservation. But much of this has remained mere talk meant to keep communities feeling proud while being shunted from enjoying in any meaningful way the cake baked from and on this heritage.

No one, particularly among the conservationists of the European extraction and their evangelical sidekicks, ever goes out of their way to do serious research on the traditional African conservation model for the purpose of incorporating some of its salient features into their conservation agenda. On their part, the national conservation agencies— —the Kenya Wildlife Service, the Kenya Forestry Service, the National Environment Management Authority, or even the parent Environment, Water & Natural Resources Ministry—have also continued to pay such hollow commendation to the contribution made by local communities in wildlife preservation and conservation.

Consequently, the role that the traditions and cultural conservation ethics of those such as the Maasai, Samburu, Rendille, Meru, and Mijikenda played in conserving the wide wildlife diversity in Kenya is never given any meaningful consideration. The way modern conservationists go about it, one might be forgiven to believe that had they not done what they say they have been doing, Kenya would not have any animals left to conserve.

The European conservation philosophy and practice is taken as if it was what was ordered of humanity by nature or God himself.

Are Traditional African Conservation Ethics Any Longer Feasible?

This is a question that is yet to be exhaustively examined in Kenya, mostly because it would necessitate the questioning of many long-held beliefs and would inevitably upset the power structures, if not the direction of the flow of donor money, and thereby threaten the vested interests that have dominated conservation in Kenya for more than one hundred years. This line of thinking is studiously avoided by conservation practitioners, despite the obvious fact that all the wildlife we are so proud of wouldn't have continued to exist in the absence of indigenous conservation ethics. Occasionally, however, some brave thinkers choose to ask this pertinent question.

To date, some Kenyan communities have upheld deep symbolism that has aided in enabling them to live and let wildlife live. This includes the Samburu people of northern Kenya who, for instance, still regard elephants as moral beings that should not be owned or exploited. This is a theme carried by Onesmus Kahindi (also known as Kahindi Lekalhaile) who demonstrates through research that to the Samburu, elephants are respected animals whose placenta harbours good fortune:

> When Samburu find an elephant skeleton, they show it the same respect [as they show] for the human dead, *asai*, by placing a green twig or stone or smearing ochre on the elephant's skull. The performer says a short blessing [not a prayer] when performing the rite. The blessing's intro depends on age group. *My child* [for elders], *my brother* [for warriors and boys], *my sister* [for maidens], *I have seen you. Sleep in peace.* Samburu believe that an elephant's placenta . . . is a harbinger of good luck and prosperity. The placenta is transported home using a donkey and buried in the homestead right in the middle of the cattle

enclosure. A few days after the burial, many white insects known as *nkurui* [no English or Latin term was found] emerge as the placenta decomposes. At the end of it, the homestead prospers and the man who buried it becomes very rich indeed.

Further, the Samburu perceive elephants as individuals and individual groups with distinct characters and identities rather than collectively as populations. "The people regard elephants as moral beings capable of hurting and being hurt. As a result, elephants attain a higher moral status in the Samburu society than any other animal, including livestock," Kahindi says.

To their credit, the Samburu have retained this perception and set of beliefs to date. Poaching, law enforcement, and conservation endeavours by different NGOs that have pitched tent in Samburu country over the last forty years have not changed it in any major way. The community finds it strange whenever anyone, government agencies included, put a claim on elephant ownership; anyone claiming to own elephants is in fact imposing a form of slavery and exploitation on the pachyderms. "To Samburu, owning a moral being is immoral or constitutes an immorality and therefore conscripts 'the being' to a lower moral order," Kahindi says.

This theme is discussed further, albeit from different angles, by Dr. John Waithaka, who says that each of the forty-two Kenyan ethnic groups developed their own unique values, language, and practices. Such values led to the development of norms, rules, and practices "that achieved sustainable resource use within their environments." As Dr. Waithaka says, such regulations were mainly based on long-term, empirical knowledge acquired from experiences, observations, and practices over countless generations and were mainly adapted to local conditions and embraced local variation.

In nearly all these cultures, the responsibility for enforcing community regulations was vested in the elders, who were empowered to exercise control over the land and prevent over-exploitation. Village councils were established to settle disputes over use of resources and that inculcated a universal respect for the environment. "From childhood, people were taught to respect nature and the world around them," Dr. Waithaka says. Wild animals were used on a sustainable basis for the provision of food, clothing, shelter, medicine, weapons, and other needs, including tribal ceremonies and rituals.

Some traditional natural resource management approaches were based on a belief system that prescribed measures that restrained people from excessive resource use. For instance, it was a taboo to kill an animal without cause. In cultures that hunted wild animals for food, wildlife was regarded as common property until killed or captured by a hunter. The hunters were themselves prohibited from taking more than was necessary for survival, lest a bad omen befell not just themselves but the whole community resulting in natural disasters such as drought, famine, and disease.

Dr. Waithaka says that some pastoralist cultures regarded wild animals as "second cattle" and could not hunt them for food except during periods of drought when cattle were scarce. He further says that each group related with the environment in distinct ways and was able to sustain ecologically viable resource management systems with considerable success: "Wildlife featured prominently in most cultural activities, ceremonies, and folklore. In most communities, folklore based on various aspects of wildlife was an important mode of imparting cultural and social norms and morals to the youth." Some animals were recognised as community totems and were protected from any form of destruction. Some myths forbade the hunting, killing, or interference with certain animals, their young, or habitats. Other myths despised the use of some resource types and looked down upon cultures that used them. For example, some cultures considered it a taboo to eat fish, birds, primates, or certain species of mammals, while others valued them greatly as food sources. Such cultural differences ensured the survival of certain species across regions where they were revered or exploited to greater or lesser extents.

This was a concept championed by Kariuki Thuku before his death in 2010. Thuku was a happy-go-lucky and extremely bright and innovative young man. Hailing from the Karima area of Othaya in Nyeri County, Thuku would find enough reason to be tickled and angered at the same time by the naiveté, deceit, and inappropriateness governing the philosophy and practice of conservation in Kenya. Between exuberant laughter and serious work, the tall, slightly built Thuku loved his drink. He was also an established organiser who worked closely with Sultan Somjee in the African Initiative for Alternative Peace & Development (AFRIPAD) before the latter relocated to Canada. Together with other AFRIPAD staff, and with financial assistance from the Gaiya Foundation, Mennonites, and other donors, the two came up with a project that utilised the rich peace traditions prevalent among many Kenyan communities to start an environment and peace initiative under the banner of the Peace Tree Project. (This was at a time when politically inspired violence and gangland executions by organised criminal networks ravaged Kenya leading to the deaths of hundreds in some of Nairobi's low-income residential estates, the Rift Valley, North Rift, and the northeastern regions of Kenya.) To Thuku, communities could learn from nature through ecoliteracy, which he believed was a strong learning mode that advances sustainable procurement of the living wisdom of the earth through intuitive means.

When Somjee and Thuku parted ways, Kariuki joined his brother, Muthee Thuku, and others to found the Porini Association that took up some of the AFRIPAD's programs. With financial support from the GEF Small Grants Programme and partnership with the National Museums of Kenya, Thuku embarked on an indigenous conservation initiative with no parallels that partly involved facilitating elders from different communities .

The elders would sit together for roundtable discussions that helped them to remember ancient places of worship and other traditional sacred sites that were held in awe by their communities centuries before and decades after the British had compromised traditional belief structures during their colonial misadventure in Kenya. The elders would then be encouraged to physically identify the exact locations of such sites, which they would later map out on topographical sheets provided by the Porini Association. For several years before he passed on, Thuku enabled the elders to unearth and reignite their memories and to lead other members of their communities in reestablishing the significance that their forebears held for such natural shrines. With Thuku's direction and assistance, the old men, and a sprinkling of women, would meet, identify, debate, argue, but later agree on the location and significance of different sacred sites.

John Mbaria, who befriended Thuku in 2003, covered several elder meetings at Karima Hill in Othaya Town in August 2007 and later in Giitune Forest in Meru County. At Karima, Mbaria met forty elders drawn from the counties of Laikipia, Meru, and Nyeri who had congregated for a unique one-week mapping initiative of the Karima Forest. Among the elders present was Mzee Kiuri Kimaru, a portly man of eighty-five who had witnessed the constant desecration of sacred sites surrounding Karima Hill since childhood and the subsequent disappearance of most of the twenty-six streams that emanated from the 265-acre forest.

"We have lost twenty streams here, and this is not the end," Mzee Kiuri told Mbaria in an interview that Mbaria later published in the *Sunday Nation*. Mzee Kiuri, who could not reconcile with the deliberate shortsightedness of public institutions to whom the management of natural resources was assigned by, and on behalf of, Kenyan citizens. He talked with mixed measures of anger and sadness as he castigated the former Othaya Town Council for destroying the indigenous vegetation in Karima Forest and replacing it with an intense cropping of an unholy mixture of eucalyptus, *Grevilles robusta*, and cedar trees. These are exotic species brought into Kenya by the British and are constantly cut to feed furnaces in a local tea factory.

"The elders are here to help the community to reestablish necessary historical and spiritual connection with the local resources," Thuku had said, explaining that he was drawn to the approach because modern conservation systems had failed to safeguard resources that are extremely important to the survival of millions of Kenyans. As Mzee Kiuri and fellow elders recounted, forests are not merely sources of water, food, and fuel; they were once held with such reverence that people had for centuries feared to destroy trees. In Othaya, this included the site where the original settler in Karima Forest, Mbaire, and his wife Nyakaguku, were buried.

As Mzee Kiuri could recall, from the hilly forest once flowed twenty-six streams with crystal clear water. But the desecration of Mbaire's final resting place, and later destruction of the forest by the British to deny hideouts to Mau Mau fighters, had led to a situation in which Karima only remotely resembled what was once a source of pride and livelihood for Mbaire's descendants. The destruction had worsened once the former Othaya Town Council assumed ownership and later leased eighty acres to a local tea factory. As a result, only six of the original streams carried any water along their courses by the time Mbaria visited the area. The rest were no more, and farmers had planted maize, beans, and other crops where water once flowed. But it was eucalyptus that had made away with much of the water because—as it was found by researchers at the World Agroforestry Centre in 2006—a mature eucalyptus sucks up as much as 200 litres of water each day. Owing to its greed for water, the tree, a native of Australia, has been used to drain swamps and marshy areas in many parts of the world.

Today, gigantic eucalyptus trees and other thirsty exotic (European) tree species dominate not just the Karima area but other ridges on the slopes of Mount Kenya, which is arguably the most significant ecosystem in the country and forms the headwaters of two of the country's most important river systems—the Tana and Ewaso. After modern farming techniques were introduced to the region, the result has been the disappearance of many springs and the muddying of key rivers such as the Gura, Thagana, and other tributaries of the Tana with high levels of silt, giving the water a continuous brown colour. In the entire area, loss of streams and natural vegetation is directly correlated with worsening seasonal droughts occasioned by climate change. And until very recently, when geothermal power generation overtook hydroelectric power in national importance, the network of streams from Mount Kenya had remained the source of about 70 percent of hydroelectric power generated in the country besides supplying millions of citizens with water.

Mount Kenya is also where a sizeable chunk of the country's commercial agriculture, such as tea, coffee, and horticulture, and a significant number of tourism outfits are based. But since the colonial period, the importance of Mount Kenya has increasingly been affected by senseless destruction, the application of inappropriate farming techniques, and the intensification of farming to provide food for a burgeoning human population. To this sad situation is added the shrinking of the age-old glaciers on top of Mount Kenya, which have lost 82 percent of their area in the last century. Scientists from the Intergovernmental Panel on Climate Change expect the mountain to lose its entire ice cover in the next thirty years.

But what became clear as Mbaria covered the elders' initiative was that Kenya does not need experts nurtured on the European education system to realize the danger that inappropriate human-environment relations and practices have and continue to pose to human survival or to offer effective and working solutions. These elder, formally uneducated men and women, whose cognitive abilities remain broadly unacknowledged, can not only clearly identify the danger but can also analyze its roots and provide solutions the West can never offer to Africa.

As the elders told Mbaria, the solution to Africa's growing environmental mess lies in returning the wildlife resources not just to their rightful owners (in Karima this would be the 10,000 or so members of the house of Mbaire) but also in giving local people an opportunity to reestablish their cultural, spiritual, and historical interconnectedness with these resources. To the late Kariuki

Thuku, the communal mapping of cultural and vital ecological sites was the beginning of a long road to reclaiming and rehabilitating forests and other resources, as well as retaining their sanctity across the country. Thuku's push was later adopted by the Kivulini Trust and other groups that have been implementing it with communities inhabiting upper eastern and northern Kenya

Apparently, though it is demonized by the West and certain local experts, returning to a traditional African conservation model and ensuring that it is devoid of the European, money-oriented approach might be part of the long-awaited solution to the management of natural commons in Kenya and elsewhere in Africa. For it is a model that has and continues to work perfectly well in many areas of Kenya, including Giitune Forest in Meru County, Loita Forest in Narok County, Mukogondo Forest in Laikipia County, and the Kaya Forests along the Kenyan coast. At a time when forests such as on Mount Kenya, the Mau Forest Complex, the Aberdares, and others (along with the biodiversity therein) have continued to either dwindle or be protected through a most ridiculous and expensive European-inspired guns-and-sanctions model, forests managed using the African conservation model are arguably the best well-preserved natural resources in Kenya.

Though the role of elders in most communities is waning, they still have substantial say on the management of some natural resources, especially among pastoralist communities. Interestingly, all relevant councils of elders, such as the famous Njuri Ncheke Meru Council of Elders, need do is educate local people and remind them of the cultural significance of the forests, and perhaps even impose powerful curses on anyone hell-bent on destroying them. Then they could leave forests and in-house species to their own devices. No one, not even the most daring of criminals, would dare go against such curses. The resultant sanctions are said to be too grave to contemplate—not just for the culprit but also their lineage.

4 ~ White Corruption in African Conservation

The need for Caucasian validation: In its promotional
stickers, all the biodiversity, landscape, and intrinsic values of
Kora National Park escape the KWS. Only the fact that one
George Adamson lived there seems to matter.
(©Mordecai Ogada)

The nature and content of current discourse on conservation
rarely allows for the use of the words white, corruption, and
conservation together in any context. Firstly, because conservation
in Africa has built around itself the well-worn aura of altruism and
absence of any material gain therefrom. When corruption occurs in
this sector, it is never addressed as such and is covered up by a
society desperate to hang on to the mythical romantic story of the
selfless conservationist, like the late George Adamson for example.
It therefore becomes *white* like white lies, which are often known to
be untruths but are never overtly addressed or accepted as such.
The misdirection, misallocation, and misuse of corporate resources
to serve various personal interests has gone on in Africa for many
generations, as it no doubt has in all human societies around the
world. In Africa, this vice really came into its own with the
establishment of countries, currencies, structured economies, and
the realization of the value of her natural resources during the
much-vaunted scramble for Africa's resources during the
nineteenth century.

The wave of independence that swept across Africa in the
latter half of the twentieth century ushered in indigenous
governments composed of local elites who had learned well at the

feet of the colonial governments. They took avarice, selfishness, cruelty, discrimination, and general graft to unprecedented levels. Even as they did this, they thumped their own chests and were revered by ignorant local populations for their role in winning freedom for their people. In Kenya, these so-called freedom fighters stepped ably into the space left by the colonizers. But in Kenya, and many parts of Africa, the one place the colonizers never moved out of (and the natives never sought for themselves) was the biodiversity sector, encompassing the conservation, consumptive, and nonconsumptive use of this resource.

There is a cultural background to this attitude that is apparent when one closely examines most preindustrial tropical African societies. Most food and energy resources were hunted or gathered, with the only constraints being the difficulty in handling the resources with the implements available at the time. Resources were abundant, and their availability was essentially constant due to the absence of seasonality. Unlike temperate lands, tropical Africa doesn't have significant variations in day length, temperatures, and natural resource availability throughout the year. In preindustrial temperate lands, natural resources had to be planned for, managed, conserved, gathered in bulk, stored, preserved and traded. This was essential in order for people to survive from the boom of summer against the deprivation brought about by the onset of winter. It was a matter of life and death, and only those who could do this survived and went on to colonize tropical lands. In tropical Africa, those who fished, hunted, and gathered edible plants did so throughout the year for generations. Very rarely was there need to store these resources or plan even days ahead, much less months or seasons. For this reason, too, we took only what we needed for whatever purpose for the present.

In temperate zones, the vast difference in climatic conditions between seasons means that many species can only reproduce and thrive within a three-month window every year. Entire populations are therefore sustained by brief, frenetic booms during which even the other species that exploit them are overwhelmed by the abundance. Examples of these are the massive movements and concentrated calving seasons of reindeer and bison in Europe and North America, respectively, as well as the massive salmon runs when the fish move upstream to spawn. This possibly gave rise to the concept of sport hunting or fishing, where having met their nutritional requirements, human societies started to kill for recreational purposes.

Over time, this evolved from a purely recreational pursuit into a much-sought channel for self-actualization where it became important to kill the rarer, more dangerous species, and even within those confines, it was more important to kill the biggest. Sport fishing also followed a similar trajectory, with extra attention being paid to species that are aggressive and fight the fisherman harder and longer, and a higher premium is placed on the larger individuals within a species. The emphasis on size is purely for self-actualization, since these animals are rarely eaten. Indeed in sport fishing, the fish are often released after weighing and measuring for record purposes.

In precolonial Africa, killing for sport was unknown, and anathema in some societies, since it was seen as an affront to the deities that provided the resource. Hunting or fishing as a pastime was, and still is, a pursuit restricted to children, and even so, the small birds and fish thus obtained are often roasted and eaten *in situ* as part of the whole activity. The ubiquitous nature of wildlife and the regularity of interaction with humans resulted in an ambivalence towards wildlife that persists to this day. This was quickly overtaken and overshadowed by the breathless fascination of those who arrived in Africa and found wildlife whose diversity, abundance, and fecundity was far beyond anything they had experienced in their homelands. This fascination came with people who already had in their psyche the need to manage wildlife, plan for wildlife, and exploit wildlife for fulfillment higher up the hierarchy of human needs.

The ambivalence of the natives and the fascination of the foreigners with wildlife respectively survived the advent of independence in African nations and the indigenization of socio-political structures that followed shortly thereafter. In postcolonial Kenya, and much of Sub-Saharan Africa, these attitudes grew and morphed into more complex and entrenched cultures around wildlife conservation and management. The native ambivalence became a vacuum in policy and the absence of an indigenous ownership or identity concerning wildlife. (In Kenya, this is evident from the ad hoc and reactive manner with which conservation challenges are dealt by the statutory authorities.) And with the development of travel, media, and information technology, the numbers of foreigners indulging in a fascination with wildlife, actually and vicariously, have risen exponentially.

This in turn has created conservationists out of people whose only claims to this role are their foreign origins and contact with and apparent concern for certain species and their habitats. Not many of these self-styled conservationists achieve the mythical hero status detailed earlier in this book, but a vast majority of them come to be considered infallible. Most of them have no formal training in ecology or conservation practices and make glaring errors in their execution, most of which are accepted by an adoring public as daring adventures. Their stories are devoured by millions the world over and are responsible for inspiring a huge amount of interest in wildlife, wild lives, and wild places. These people bask in the glory of their (mis)deeds during their lifetimes, and their reputations over the generations survive actions that would invite intense odium in their own countries.

A prime example of this phenomenon is the late Gerald Durrell. He is so highly regarded a naturalist as to have a premier conservation and ecology institution in his name. The Durrell Institute of Conservation and Ecology (DICE) in Canterbury is the largest academic institute dedicated to conservation in the UK and has trained thousands of conservation practitioners from all over the world at graduate and postgraduate levels. This institute "sets itself apart from more traditionally minded academic institutions with its clear mission." This mission includes breaking down the barriers between the natural and social sciences in conservation, building natural resource management capacity with a focus in biodiversity rich developing countries, and a focus on scientific research that informs practical implementation. This institutional mission comprises the three most important ingredients lacking in conservation practice and study in Africa, and it follows that this institution is likely to be making a significant positive impact on conservation worldwide.

However, the practices of Gerald Durrell were far from being in line with the mission of the DICE. The activities and adventures detailed in Gerald Durrell's books aren't those of a conservationist by any stretch of the definition. He was an animal collector who visited various countries to collect rare and exotic animals simply for the pleasure of having the specimens as his own. There is no evidence in any of his books of affinity to *in situ* conservation of the species he apparently cared so much about or formal engagement with statutory authorities on the same.

Durrel's books read like casual jaunts into the uncivilized bush to collect anything cute, rare, or otherwise attractive to him, which is probably the reason why they resonated with the childhood fantasies of many the world over and made him famous. The attitude Durrell had towards Africans as illustrated in his books is paternalistic at best, with a dehumanizing tone and attitude running through his entire body of work. A case in point is the *Bafut Beagles* in which the title of this book is used as a term not only to describe the packs of mongrels deployed by Durrell to hunt down hapless wildlife but includes the African hunters who accompanied him and owned said dogs. Western audiences of wildlife enthusiasts are generally insensible of such casual disrespect of local African peoples but are uniformly vigorous defenders of the welfare of African animals. In all reviews and critiques of Durrell's works, there is no mention of the myriad animal welfare issues arising from the use of dogs to bay animals up trees or the lighting of fires to smoke monkeys out of trees among other unenlightened practices.

The veritable armies of animal welfare advocates in the West are conspicuous here by their silence about his activities. In one of his chronicles of animal collecting expeditions, he details how he smuggled a mongoose home. There is not a single question that has been raised about why he was carrying a young (extremely rare) black-footed mongoose in his shirt or who he was concealing it from. Just admiration for how he endured scratches on his stomach and amusement at the mongoose's urine stains on his shirt. The Gerald Durrell phenomenon is just one example of the infallibility of the perceived altruistic conservationist so firmly entrenched in the collective psyche of the wildlife conservation audience. It is the basis upon which white corruption in the conservation sector thrives and flourishes, unencumbered by mundane concerns like taxation, accountability, labour laws, human rights, intellectual property rights, and animal welfare. To his credit, Durrell never went overboard in trying to hide the nature of his activities. His attitude towards capture, transportation, and keeping exotic animals is illuminated by the title of one of his more popular works, *A Zoo in My Luggage*.

Kenya has long been regarded (rightly or wrongly) as a world leader in conservation practice. This view hasn't been driven by any extraordinary achievements in practice or levels of scholarship but by this country being at a confluence of different factors that have helped it capture the world's imagination over the years. These include its stunning parks and biodiversity, tropical climate, aggressive capitalism, large expatriate population, vibrant tourism sector, and more than its fair share of charismatic story-tellers in the conservation scene. The combination of these and other factors have created a matrix in Kenyan conservation through which white corruption thrives, because the entire world so desperately needs to believe the romantic myths that are created around conservation in Kenya and relentlessly burnished by its tourism industry. In conservation, doublespeak and obfuscations are commonplace in the pursuit of personal acclaim or material gain. However, in Kenyan conservation practice, white corruption has been institutionalized, posing the greatest threat to our wildlife and natural resources.

Bioprospecting is one field in which Kenya has borne the brunt of white corruption to a level where it is barely understood to be the biopiracy that it is. The earliest of well-known examples is the case of the drug Acarbose, a glucosidase inhibitor commonly used in the treatment of type 2 diabetes and marketed by the German pharmaceutical giant Bayer. The patent on its manufacture was filed by Bayer and issued in Europe, the US, and Australia in 1997. This patent reveals that an *Actinoplanes sp.* bacteria strain called SE 50 has unique genes that enable the biosynthesis of Acarbose in fermenters. The strain comes from Kenya's Lake Ruiru. In 2001 in an article in the *Journal of Bacteriology*, a group of Bayer scientists and German academics confirmed that SE 50 was being used to manufacture Acarbose. The article fully describes the manufacturing process of Acarbose and related compounds but tactfully makes no mention of Kenya or Africa.

However, the article does expressly say, "The oral antidiabetic agent [Acarbose] is produced by fermentation of the actinomycete *Actinoplanes sp.* strain SE50." This is the same strain that is identified as Kenyan in the patent application filed six years before. As of December 31, 2004, Bayer sales of Acarbose totaled €278 million ($379 million). As a statutory authority in Kenya, the KWS is supposed to be the custodian of Kenya's biological resources. It is well-known that the KWS's precursor was the Game Department, which in turn was formed primarily to manage Kenya's populations of megafauna, so there is nothing in the institution's history that would prepare them to address issues like companies bioprospecting in Kenya for microbes. However, the concept of biodiversity and ecosystems isn't novel, and the law giving the KWS the mandate to manage it is decades old. And this organization has thus far failed to adjust itself to the new challenges of managing and protecting all of Kenya's biodiversity, of which wildlife is but a small fraction.

There are no laboratories of any kind at the KWS, much less those equipped with the materials and capacity to meet these new challenges. In an attempt to manage biodiversity research, there are thousands of research permits and attached proposals lodged at the National Council for Science and Technology in Nairobi every year, and further permits are issued by the KWS based on whether a researcher will be handling animals or working in a protected area. All of these applications and documents, however, are reviewed, stored and handled by administrative and clerical staff who aren't capable of assessing their legal and scientific merit or lack thereof. Research permitting is still treated in Kenya as a collection process for petty taxes.

The Kenya Wildlife Service still doesn't have an institutional research agenda, despite having scores of personnel on its payroll referred to as scientists. The one attempt by the KWS to get payment for use of Kenya's biological resources is a prime example of how not to manage a people's heritage and birthright. In 2007, the KWS unveiled a biotechnology research agreement with the world's top industrial enzymes maker, the Danish company Novozymes, and vowed to go after biopirates accused of plundering Kenya's rich natural resources. This agreement was to govern the use of enzymes developed from microbes in Kenya's Rift Valley soda lakes as a key ingredient of products ranging from detergent and bleach used in the manufacture of denim apparel to animal feed.

The KWS was very proud of this agreement, and then director Dr. Julius Kipngetich is quoted as saying, "The KWS-Novozymes partnership provides a new avenue for formal exploitation of Kenya's microbial diversity, whose potential has largely been unexploited." Novozymes now has the right to market products developed from Kenyan microorganisms in return for one-off discovery payments, facilities, and training for Kenyan researchers.

The KWS acted like the owner rather than the caretaker of this national resource, entering into an agreement that would earn far less than what any country should be paid by a foreign interest wanting patents or exclusive use of any of said country's natural resources. The final insult in this litany of resource robbery was a payment from Novozymes of 2.3 million Kenyan shillings (approximately $26,500) as royalties out of the millions of dollars earned from the products of these microbes. The Baringo County governor, Benjamin Cheboi, presided over the ceremony that handed over this princely sum and proudly crowed that "communities had every right to benefit from the resources." Apparently, the KWS saw this tragedy as some kind of victory to be reveled in, with the assistant director, Michael Kipkeu, giving a warning to other people purporting to do research in Kenya while taking away resources for commercial gain. It is difficult to imagine starker evidence of the intellectual vacuum that exists in the structures that are supposed to manage natural resources on behalf and for the benefit of the Kenyan people.

Western biodiversity buccaneers have been at work in Africa for a long time. For example, in the 1970s, there were claims that a muddy substance found in Lang'o District in Uganda had the power to heal a number of ailments. However, local healthcare officials and other experts dismissed these claims as unsubstantiated rumours put about by witchdoctors. However, as detailed in a new report published by a US think-tank, *Out of Africa: Mysteries of Access and Benefit Sharing*, a British company, SR Pharma (formerly Stanford Rook Ltd.), took the prejudged rumours seriously. After intensive research, the company ended up isolating a unique bacterium, *Microbacterium vaccae*, that is now used effectively against chronic viral infections, including HIV. Needless to say, SR Pharma made millions of dollars in annual sales and, according to the report, never saw any reason for sharing a single shilling with those who came up with the initial claims.

There are numerous other examples of skin care products, appetite suppressants, and other pharmaceuticals that come from natural sources and are identified by indigenous knowledge in Africa. For so many years, our Eurocentric education model taught us that anything indigenous was heresy, witchcraft, or folktales. It is a stunning turnaround that now sees the same Europeans recognizing and relentlessly exploiting this indigenous knowledge only matched by Africans' intellectually vacuous obeisance to the exotic models of education that have excluded their indigenous knowledge for so long.

The chicanery that swirls around microbiology and the development of chemicals is arguably easy to conceal from scrutiny. This is because microbes and chemicals are generally known only to specialists, because the lay person cannot see, smell, synthesize, or even recognise them for what they are. White corruption, however is not limited to the specialist sector. It also extends into the realm of activities that are generally well understood by all. For example, the blatant misuse of community needs and worldwide concern for wildlife conservation for individual profit.

In Kenya, single-species-focused organizations styled as charities and nonprofit organizations are raking in hundreds of thousands of dollars by engaging in the tourism industry under the guise of conservation activities. It is a very well thought out model to get the most out of a tourist by cleverly tapping into his or her psychological needs. High-end tourism is a self-actualization pursuit, but it is a practice that is also steeped in irony, because high-end tourists to poverty-stricken areas are loath to be regarded as hedonists. Media personalities, business magnates, politicians, and others with public wealth are particularly vulnerable to this conundrum, because they perceive their success as dependent, to some level, on the way their audience perceives them. This insecurity is relentlessly exploited through white corruption all over sub-Saharan Africa, with numerous offers of ways in which one can burnish their image by spending heavily on various conservation initiatives. A typically breathless blurb on the internet reads:

JOURNEYS FOR GIANTS EXPERIENTIAL ITINERARY

A 10-Day Safari for Conservation

Space for Giants invites you to join a one-of-a-kind African adventure to experience firsthand our crucial conservation work and the magnificent animals we strive to protect. Not only will you explore the breathtaking landscapes of Laikipia, you will also experience African cultures, search for the 'Big Five,' and enjoy access to our leading conservationists and researchers striving to secure the future for Africa's giants.

The above advertisement is accompanied by a detailed itinerary informing the visitor of all the people they will meet, places they will visit, and activities they will participate in. For this package, the 2013 price was $5,200 per person based on a group of four and $5,000 per person based on a group of six to eight. Those in the safari business will recognise these as falling within the typical price range for this kind of product. However, in this case there are also mandatory donations with a precisely calculated and prescribed minimum. Every guest must pay a donation of $3,750 per person for four adults, $2,000 per person for six adults, or $1,250 per person for eight adults. Still, there isn't any apparent impropriety in this arrangement. Besides, the donations are willingly given by people who must subscribe to whatever Space for Giants tells them.

The legal lacuna is where the organization is registered abroad as a charity and in Kenya as a conservation research outfit but in actual fact operates as a competitive player in the local tourism sector. The charity registration abroad allows well-heeled guests to give with significant tax advantages, and the conservation research tag actually gives Space for Giants a strong competitive edge, because it allows much closer (literally hands-on) access to elephants than the standard safari outfit. Most importantly, it allows the organization to duck all the regulations that govern typical tour operators, including off-road driving, licensing, registration, and taxation. By this, and all other indications, elephants are not only of monetary value to poachers and ivory smuggling gangs. This species is relentlessly exploited and is only endangered because so little of what it earns for so many organizations, such as Space for Elephants, actually goes towards its conservation.

Elephant profiteering schemes are numerous and cannot be faulted for lack of creativity. A flyer on the website of the Amboseli Trust for Elephants (ATE) states (again in typically breathless fashion):

> Our Program is Unique. Each Amboseli elephant is known to us as an *individual* and, at birth, is given a code name based on his or her mother's name and year of birth. At about four years of age, we give each calf a real name, according to family. Each calf is named only once and the name stays with that calf for life. For a donation of US $2,500, you can name an Amboseli calf in honour of someone special in your life. ATE donors have already named calves after their children, grandchildren, parents, spouses, special friends and acquaintances. We have many donors who have named calves after themselves, their family name, or a beloved pet. The Amboseli Calf Naming Program is unique. It differs from other "naming and adoption" programs in which tens or even hundreds of donors are invited to name or adopt the same animal. Our program is exclusive. The calf you name will be named by you only and the name will stay with that calf for life. It will also be recorded in all research project documents, where it will be used forever. The Calf Naming Program is a perfect way to honour someone special in your life with a truly unique gift.

The reader is exhorted to give a donation in order to have someone go out into the bush and name a *wild* animal according to his or her wishes. This net is cast wide enough to capture all the needs and foibles of the wealthy, including hubris, need for validation, tight family ties, loving memories, self-actualization, hedonism, and simple feel-good gratification. The clincher here is the simple sale (at a premium price) of a completely intangible and practically inexhaustible commodity. There are around 14,000 elephants in Amboseli, so there are thousands of calves available, and best of all, when you name a calf, it doesn't get branded or otherwise labelled as belonging to the customer.

The white corruption field is now getting pretty crowded, unlike the good old days when Africa was a place of untold suffering and there were only a few legendary intrepid souls willing to sacrifice everything to work in conservation. In the Amboseli Trust for Elephants blurb there is evidence that can attest to this fact, for example the reference to "other naming and adoption programs" where the ATE claims that "tens or even hundreds" are invited to adopt or name the same animal. Currently, there are only two elephant calf naming and adoption programs in Kenya, so this is a thinly veiled reference to the one other, which is run by the David Sheldrick Wildlife Trust based in Nairobi National Park.

Here, it is a different model: Elephant calves are brought in from all over the country, wherever they may have been found orphaned or separated from their family herds. At a facility, the calves are hand-fed and cared for by dedicated assistants, often brought back from death's door, since many are in extremely poor condition when brought in. The quality and quantity of food needed to raise an elephant calf from infancy to adolescence presents a daunting financial outlay to any individual, and to her credit, Dame Dr. Daphne Sheldrick has managed to mobilize considerable resources over the years to meet such needs. The orphanage opens to the public during the elephants' exercise hour and offers visitors an extremely moving spectacle. A line of baby elephants appears walking from the holding pens, accompanied by their keepers, and make their way towards a large mud hole. The young calves throw themselves into the mud and water with abandon, frolicking in obvious enjoyment. Any adult with the slightest affinity for wildlife is deeply moved, and for children, it is nothing short of a life-changing experience. The coup de grâce is when the orphans are led around the restraining ropes close

118

enough for the visitors to touch them and for them to extend their trunks for a good sniff at said visitors. The one-hour session is long enough to make people fall in love with these orphans but nowhere near long enough for visitors to have their fill of the experience, so when they are informed on their way out that they can buy a t-shirt, make a donation, or even adopt and name an elephant calf, they are truly captivated.

The amount donors are asked for is supposedly based on the costs of rearing these elephant calves to adolescence, so the substantial amount is immediately justified. The donor also understands that these are recurrent costs and expects to donate regularly. The immediate challenge, of course, is the fact that this facility hosts less than thirty orphaned elephants at a time, and there are hundreds of enthralled visitors coming to see them every day and wanting to name and sponsor the little jumbos. The only way out of this is to have multiple names and adoptions per calf, so that no naming opportunity or donation is missed. The fact that the David Sheldrick Wildlife Trust has done this, and made it work, is testimony to an admirable database management system that must necessarily keep track of who gave how much money to give which jumbo what name. The intricacy of this task becomes apparent when one considers that there are regular status and health updates, Christmas cards, birthday cards, and photographs that have to be sent to donors all over the world on the correct dates and using the correct names for the calves.

This is the grey area that the Amboseli Trust refers to snidely by calling their own naming program unique, in that they claim every calf is only named once. It is an ethically difficult arrangement to maintain, especially since it is unlikely that none of the punters from all over the world have caught on to it by simple triangulation. The David Sheldrick Wildlife Trust, however, has a trump card: the ability to let you touch, cuddle, and smell your very own elephant calf, which the ATE cannot do. On the other hand, the ATE receives donations for naming calves in whose growth and welfare the sponsor has no investment whatsoever in terms of time, energy, or money. There certainly isn't any modicum of honour among elephant calf adoption and naming programs.

Elephant conservation groups, or any group who styles themselves as such, appear to hold extraordinary sway in Kenya. Save the Elephants, the Amboseli Trust for Elephants, and the David Sheldrick Wildlife Trust are all organizations that enjoy the extraordinary privilege of having been granted permanent residence inside protected areas. A casual glance at this circumstance only reveals the logistic advantage of closeness to their field sites and study subjects (in the cases of Save the Elephants and the ATE). This is a key advantage they have been granted, or have commandeered, over any other organization wanting to do wildlife research in said areas. More than 60 percent of the average cost of a wildlife research project in Kenya is spent on just getting to the subjects, so the significance of this advantage cannot be overstated.

Those who have attempted to do wildlife research in Kenya's protected areas have always had to negotiate a byzantine process of annual permits, proposal writing, explanations, and the added expense of having to be accompanied by armed park staff, but the above lucky few do not. More importantly, their highly attractive locations are magnets for visitors, and they all engage in donor visits, which is a euphemism for informal tourism where the (unpermitted) visitors enjoy research-level access to wildlife and pay a premium fee (in the form of donations). The other tourism operators have to pay park entry fees, taxes, license fees, etc. but aren't even allowed to step out of their cars in the parks and cannot offer any such experiences to their guests.

The most insidious impact of white corruption is its gravitational pull on resources that could otherwise have a greater positive impact on wildlife conservation and the welfare of local communities living with wildlife. This doesn't occur in far-flung field locations but in luxuriously appointed offices in major cities and at glamorous, expertly marketed fund-raising events that include art competitions, off-road driving competitions, bicycle races, and marathons. The whole machine is primed to find the heart strings of animal lovers and tug them mercilessly with unadulterated doses of the plight of wildlife, the misery of people, and the selfless sacrifices of the heroes who save them in Kenya.

There are clichés that have served this cause so well over the years that their users cannot notice when they cross the thin blurred line between cliché and circus prop. The Maasai beaded regalia is a case in point. It is so heavily used in tourism, by airlines, and conservation organizations that it eclipses many other representations of Kenyan heritage, and the very meaning of the beads themselves is lost. One such instance is the Tusk Trust awards in 2013. This organization is a leading worldwide campaigner against elephant poaching and has had extraordinary success in garnering support from prominent personalities, including its patron, HRH Prince William, the Duke of Cambridge.

As one can imagine, the annual Tusk awards ceremony held in London involves a huge amount of the pomp and pageantry typical of events that involve the Royalty. The overall winner in 2013 was Tom Lalampaa, the community programs manager with the Northern Rangelands Trust. The world was treated to the spectacle of this portly gentleman dressed only in a red wraparound loincloth and rubber sandals and adorned with beads standing among the black-tie-clad Duke and officials of the trust.

Those who know Mr. Lalampaa personally can attest to the fact that he is an urbane and erudite gentleman who doesn't dress in this manner when he is at work in Samburu, where he comes from. The machine, however, needs to be fed on romantic stories of savages who have miraculously seen the light and turned into conservationists, never mind that the savages' homeland was teeming with wildlife before exotic conservation models were deemed necessary by a colonial elite.

A documentary released by the Tusk Trust detailing the efforts of the NRT in Northern Kenya included a bizarre segment of a tough, uniformed game ranger crying over a dead elephant. People familiar with the conditions and stresses of everyday life faced by young men in Samburu and the highly patriarchal Maa culture would be taken aback by this aberration. The closest comparison is probably a captive Indian sun bear dancing with a controlling ring through its nose.

The private conservation sector in Kenya is vibrant and is a strident voice against poaching and other wildlife crime. As a result, this sector takes in the majority of public and private funding that comes into the country for conservation work. However, this sector also includes wildlife conservancies that are basically privately owned and managed wildlife habitats or sanctuaries. These owners and managers have spent a lot of their own money in order to successfully appeal for considerably greater sums of money from donors to secure wildlife populations. Having done this, certain conservancies are now offering secure habitats to the KWS for rhinos, which get translocated after exhaustive inspections of said conservancies' security structures.

Interestingly, these conservancies have also undertaken to equip their own wildlife security squads with skills in firearms handling and tactical manoeuvers. This extraordinary effort was undertaken ostensibly to fill a gap in enforcement left by the KWS. However, this strategy appears to have failed spectacularly in the first quarter of 2014, with rhino killings at Ol Jogi and Ol Pejeta conservancies rapidly surpassing the totals for 2013. What, then is the purpose of these militias? These two conservancies are highly secure and known to spend hundreds of thousands of dollars every year on security, including fencing, ground patrols, and aircraft. They both have livestock production systems, and neither has ever even experienced the theft of cattle. So how poachers are claimed to have breached their defences, killed rhinos, and made off with the horns undetected remains a mystery to many.

In July 2014, none other than the Acting Kenya Wildlife Service Director, William Kiprono, warned that the KWS had evidence of collusion between poachers and the management of some wildlife conservancies. On the other hand, the KWS subsequently exposed a key institutional weakness in that they tacitly admitted to considering these community conservation practitioners to be above suspicion as regards wildlife crime because they do not need to profit from the proceeds thereof. One wonders what the basis of this consideration on the part of the KWS might be. Whether it is economic status, race, size of landholding, or any other subjective criteria, it is contrary to the mission of any law enforcement agency.

In this particular issue, the casual observer might be baffled as to how or why such an unholy alliance as between poachers and conservationists could occur. However, an insider's knowledge of the numbers game in Kenyan conservation reveals that a fifty kilogram ivory haul from a poached elephant will earn the poacher around 250,000 Kenyan shillings (approximately $2,900) while photographs of the poached and dismembered animal can earn over $100,000 in donor support for antipoaching activities. In theory, therefore, a poached elephant on a private conservancy can actually be a win-win situation for everyone. The only losers, of course, are the elephants. But in the murky field of white corruption, animals are just commodities for poachers, conservationists, and tourism operators alike.

Many incidences of white corruption appear to portray this vice as a mild irritant that can be resisted by any functioning system, simply a small cabal of tax evaders and charity sharks. The dangers it poses to wildlife populations and community cohesion, however, are disconcertingly real. This fact was rudely brought home to those privy to the machinations around the proposed amendments to Kenya's wildlife laws in December 2004.

Then member of Parliament for Laikipia West (now the senator for Laikipia County), Godfrey Gitahi (G. G.) Kariuki, brought to parliament a bill to amend the wildlife act. At a glance, the so-called G. G. Bill was meant to correct anomalies in the country's wildlife conservation policies. It said nice and welcome things on how to rationalize appointments at the Kenya Wildlife Service and sought to compel the government to raise the compensation for victims of wild animal attacks from 30,000 Kenyan shillings ($384.60) to 10 million Kenyan shillings

($128,205). This was fine news indeed, particularly to local people who had lost livelihoods, livestock, and the lives of loved ones again and again to marauding elephants, stealthy leopards, and aggressive lions. Indeed, this part of the bill was publicized ad nauseam in the local press, resulting in fulsome praise for the visionary Kariuki. However, there was a catch. Stashed away and hidden in a faraway corner of the document among the mind-numbing legalese was a clause that said the bill would do away with a presidential directive issued by Kenya's first president, Jomo Kenyatta, outlawing all hunting activities in the country. "Legal Notice No. 120 of 1977 (officially) Repealed," read the terse statement.

The drafters of the bill had the temerity to present arguments to the effect that it made no sense to continue outlawing hunting while the KWS and its predecessor, the Wildlife Conservation & Management Department (WMCD), had all along been engaged in some form of hunting through animal culling to protect crops, livestock, and property. They also claimed that by allowing game cropping, game capture, and translocation, the KWS had indeed condoned, if not encouraged, hunting. Further the bill accused the two institutions of having "consistently contravened the ban by hunting widely and for many reasons since 1977." And in parliament, Kariuki defended his motion by alluding that his bill was only seeking" to regularize all hunting that has been routinely undertaken by, or through KWS."

It was a stunning display of hubris for one to suggest that a security agency carrying out its constitutional mandate could be a justification for private profiteers to undertake similar actions. The bill was passed in parliament to the delight of sport hunting interests and the horror of animal welfare groups. However, the celebrations were cruelly cut short when then President Mwai Kibaki refused to sign the bill into law as was his constitutional prerogative.

There are many theories as to why Kibaki rejected this bill, but his action spared Kenya an apocalypse. How the prohunting lobbyists expected to legalize killing wildlife for sport while others were being arrested for subsistence hunting was anybody's guess. Kenyan law maintains very tight control of firearms, so this law was mainly to benefit a small Kenyan elite and their foreign clientele. How did Kenya reach the edge of this precipice? The answer may lie in a few facts that seem minor at first glance.

Firstly, the bill was passed very late in the evening, around 9:00 p.m. This is significant to any observer familiar with the extraordinary sloth that typically characterized the activities of Kenya's Tenth Parliament. Secondly, the extended all-expenses paid tour of Southern Africa by the MPs, ostensibly to see the benefits of consumptive use of wildlife. Thirdly, G. G. Kariuki's membership in the Laikipia Wildlife Forum, a group then conducting zebra cropping as an experimental way of landowners to profit from wildlife on their land. White corruption had shown sharp teeth and powerful muscle. Kenya's conservation sector barely survived the onslaught.

A white lie is defined by the MacMillan dictionary as an untruth told to avoid upsetting someone else, not for the liar's own advantage or in order to harm someone else. In a similar manner, white corruption is graft that we accept in order to protect our own belief in the heroes, myths, and legends we have created and hold so dear. The perpetration of white lies is always a very short-lived solution because there is always a human party to whom the perpetrator will be ultimately accountable. In the conservation sector, however, this party is a voiceless ecosystem, species, national park, or even an individual animal who cannot call the perpetrator to account.

Sadly, this has now expanded to include communities who have been bombarded with handouts, awareness campaigns, and occasionally the sheer force of an individual's charisma into forgetting that they had an identity and a way of life that existed before Western conservation arrived. Our statutory authority, the Kenya Wildlife Service, has perfected the dumb-gunbearer role, as illustrated by the alacrity with which they have invited a former colleague of George Adamson's, Tony Fitzjohn, to come and revive Kora National Park. This initiative was detailed in the *Sunday Nation* newspaper of September 7, 2014, under the awestruck heading "Incomparable." This invitation is based in the firm belief that Kora only exists because of the late George Adamson and that the KWS is incapable of managing or marketing it and the belief that the beautiful landscapes and wildlife have no intrinsic value beyond that of a white man living there.

Kenya has plumbed new intellectual depths by trying to replace Adamson, because even as we ascribe some quasi-messianic status to him, we don't ascribe that quality to him individually, and we assume another from the same stock will duplicate what we had in Adamson. The uncomfortable truth is that white corruption is the term that most accurately describes at least 95 percent of the private or civil society conservation sector in sub-Saharan Africa today. Its ubiquity across the continent is only matched by how deeply entrenched it is in practice and study.

Multi-million-dollar organizations, scores of major policy decisions, thousands of careers, thousands of scientific publications and degrees, and the moral satisfaction of millions of people have been built on white corruption in conservation. To challenge this animal is widely considered to be heresy and treated as such. Professionally, it can be very detrimental to job security and career progress, and before attempting to do so, all who think they want to challenge it must understand that bursting this particular bubble will be far more than upsetting an apple-cart. It will be a revolution that will bring about as many ends as it will beginnings.

Naturally, such a revolution will be fought by the status quo with everything they have. However, we are all being driven towards this endgame by forces that are far beyond the control of any individual. These include the flow of information, the penetration of information technology, the exchange of ideas, and the opening of minds. An inescapable irony is the role that white corruption itself will have played in this revolution. The bursaries thrown in as part of the pittances paid to communities to sign away their land have resulted in a small but influential group of educated young people in these wildlife areas. Additionally, the endless conservation awareness campaigns used to fritter away donor funds have brought people together and opened these communities' eyes to the incredible monetary, intrinsic, and cultural value of their birthright and the resources they have lived with for generations.

5 ~ Debunking the Myths

The need to maintain a crisis: Unsubstantiated figures like "100 elephants are killed in Africa every day" are a crucial tool in a culture of relentless begging, as seen in this poster at a supermarket in Nairobi. (©Mordecai Ogada)

The origins of modern conservation practices initially came out of the fascination people have for places they cannot easily access and creatures they cannot easily see. This fascination engendered numerous myths about people, places, and species. The most persistent myths, however, have always been those that grew around the personalities involved. The reason for this is that in the days of discovery, before many of the technologies we use today, it generally required amazing feats of endurance, skill, and occasionally foolishness just to successfully undertake these adventures. The mere journey to get to a place and back to tell a story bestowed celebrity status on the explorers who braved these expeditions, immortality on those who died, and perpetual fame on those who learned and taught us something.

Examples include Charles Darwin, David Livingstone, John Muir, Robert Scott, and Henry Morton Stanley. Closer to us in space and time, we have the pioneers of African conservation, including Mervyn Cowie, George Adamson, Fredrick Selous, Archie Ritchie, Joy Adamson, and David Sheldrick, among numerous others. In most recent times, we have the likes of Richard Leakey, Jane Goodall, Daphne Sheldrick, Cynthia Moss, David Western, and Iain Douglas-Hamilton. The conservation sector has consistently honoured these individuals in word and deed for some real and some imagined contributions to the cause of conservation.

There is very little method or reason to this adulation, as certain pioneers who made significant actual contributions to natural resource conservation in Kenya are little known in literature or lore. One example of the unknowns is the person or people who conceived the idea of establishing protected areas around Mount Kenya and the Aberdare Mountains. Historical records only show that these protected areas were established through the National Parks ordinance of 1945. They were exclusively for European recreation in the form of hunting and trout fishing. The economic value of these two protected areas to Kenya in terms of urban water supplies, water for irrigation, and hydroelectricity cannot be overstated and defies calculation.

Conservation discourse today, however, is inextricably tied to the tourism industry, perpetuating the myth that blurs the line between the principles of conservation and the business interests of tourism. The persistence of this myth in twenty-first-century Kenya is an indictment of the conservation sector and betrays the shallowness of conservation thinking that pervades society. We are obsessed with the so-called charismatic species at the expense of looking after their habitats and the human communities that share them. The millions of farmers and pastoralists who share the land and resources with wildlife are largely regarded as a necessary evil, since they cannot be culled, translocated, or fenced out in order to conserve habitats strictly for wildlife and tourists.

The first myth is one that stares society in the face every day but is rarely acknowledged, even in private forums. Why are all the people who are (rightly or wrongly) hailed as great conservationists Caucasian? Surely, in approximately the last one hundred years of structured conservation practice, there must have been some indigenous effort in this realm, so the question is why no indigenous conservationists have received adulation or romanticised status. The greatest example of local recognition to an indigenous Kenyan for contributions to conservation has undoubtedly been to the late Nobel laureate Prof. Wangari Maathai. A closer look at this apparent exception to the race rule, however, will reveal that she received none of this adulation prior to her winning the Nobel Peace Prize in 2004.

Indeed, Professor Maathai wasn't really an exception to this rule, because our recognition of her in Kenya was imposed upon us by the Nobel committee in spite of our ambivalent attitude towards her and her cause. Prior to her award she was regarded by most as a rabble-rouser who was foolish enough to try and stand up to former president Daniel Arap Moi and the all-powerful Kenya African National Union (KANU) government. At that time, the most overt local support for her cause came when a group of students from Kenyatta University, outraged by a violent attack on her by progovernment thugs at Karura Forest, commandeered an assortment of vehicles, drove to Karura, and visited similar revenge on her attackers.

The alienation of indigenous Africans from the cause of conservation as currently practiced can also be seen in the array of awards received by Professor Maathai in her lifetime. These include the Sophie Prize (2004), the Petra Kelly Prize for Environment (2004), the Conservation Scientist Award (2004), the J. Sterling Morton Award (2004), the WANGO Environment Award (2003), the Outstanding Vision and Commitment Award (2002), the Excellence Award from the Kenyan Community Abroad (2001), the Golden Ark Award (1994), the Juliet Hollister Award (2001), the Jane Adams Leadership Award (1993), the Edinburgh Medal (1993), the Hunger Project's Africa Prize for Leadership (1991), the Goldman Environmental Prize (1991), the Woman of the World (1989), the Windstar Award for the Environment (1988), the Better World Society Award (1986), the Right Livelihood Award (1984), and the Woman of the Year Award (1983).

Maathai was also listed on UNEP's Global 500 Hall of Fame and named one of the one hundred heroines of the world. In June 1997, she was elected by Earth Times as one of on hundred persons in the world who have made a difference in the environmental arena and has also received honorary doctoral degrees from several institutions around the world: William's College (1990), Hobart & William Smith Colleges (1994), the University of Norway (1997), and Yale University (2004). It isn't simply the range of awards and recognitions she received that is remarkable, but the fact that not a single one is from an African institution.

An important myth about this alienation of indigenous people from modern conservation is the one that places responsibility for it solely at the feet of colonial powers, foreign scientists, tourists, and other exotic interests. These may have been its originators, but the indigenous African people and institutions are squarely to blame for the perpetuation and persistence of this alienation nearly two centuries after colonists arrived on our shores. Most indigenous Kenyans with the educational credentials to lead our conservation thinking have found material and professional comfort outside the intellectual arena where conservation policy is formulated and conservation resources are targeted. This situation is best illustrated by the resolute indifference with which the

131

government handles the offices that are supposed to govern the most precious of Kenya's natural resources.

Dr. Richard Leakey was appointed director of the Kenya Wildlife Service in 1989 with the express purposes of moulding it into a service-oriented organization and bringing then rampant poaching under control. The Kenya Wildlife Service had been created by an act of parliament to replace the Wildlife Conservation and Management Department. Leakey, a charismatic, persuasive, and driven individual, mobilized all the resources needed and took the fight to the poachers with alacrity. There was a war to be fought, and Leakey won it, deservedly cementing his place in Kenya's conservation history, despite the many weaknesses that he demonstrated as a director. Subsequent appointments to the office of the KWS director do not reflect any logic or reason at work in appointing the person in charge of Kenya's most valuable natural resource. It has just been a game of musical chairs to a discordant ethnic and political tune. The tenures of David Western, Nehemiah Rotich, Joe Kioko, Evans Mukolwe, and Michael Wamithi are remarkable for how little movement in any direction of change these directors achieved.

The growth, stability, and professionalism that were witnessed in the Kenya Wildlife Service in the years 2005-2013 under the tenure of Dr. Julius Kipng'etich were highly significant. Internally generated revenues grew from $15 million to $46 million, and there were rises of similar magnitude in the vehicle fleet, aircraft fleet, staff housing, and morale. Also, the visible image of the KWS changed drastically with rebranded parks, vehicles, and facilities. The KWS had very much arrived as an organization and won numerous corporate awards as a result. As a country, however, Kenya must necessarily temper her pride with the knowledge that this was a case of a lucky shot in the dark.

Clearly, Dr. Kipng'etich's work at the helm had nothing to do with luck, and his achievements at the KWS were the result of his considerable management skills and qualifications. These, coupled with his extraordinary intelligence and commitment to the cause of conservation, were a recipe for success. However, there wasn't any discernible structure or process by which Dr. Kipng'etich was arrived upon as the choice to run the KWS. The powers that be didn't care enough about Kenya's conservation sector to have such a process, and they stumbled on the right person who then tackled the job with skill and commitment.

The efforts of one individual eventually made Kenya look like it had a coherent conservation policy and direction, even masking the embarrassing ten-year circus that our attempts to redraft the wildlife bill had become. Dr. Kipng'etich made it his goal to make Kenya a world conservation leader, and we actually started to look the part, but all these pretensions were ruthlessly exposed when he departed the KWS in 2012 to take up a senior management position at Equity Bank. To those who know him, it seemed extremely unlikely that Dr. Kipng'etich would leave without notice to his employers, pointing to political interference fueled by the increased financial muscle of conservation players from the private sector. The confusion, deafening silence, and paralysis in the KWS that immediately followed his departure is therefore damning evidence that his appointment was a stroke of luck and not the result of a successful and objective recruitment process.

In October 2012, the head of security for the KWS, Peter Leitoro, was appointed acting director, an appointment that lasted four days before he was informed in the middle of a meeting that William Kiprono, a former county commissioner, had been given the position. Since then, poaching and wildlife crime rates in Kenya have reached the proportions of a crisis. There have been allegations of KWS staff complicity and consequent restructurings, interdictions, suspensions, investigations, and reinstatements. The organization seems to be overwhelmed, and the Cabinet Secretary has reacted by forming a task force to direct the running of the organization. This is a clear indictment of Kiprono's performance, but the KWS is bizarrely now expected to be effective with Kiprono still in office.

The apparent grace with which Dr. Kipng'etich executed his

duties as director of the KWS belies the difficulties facing this
organization as it tries to enforce conservation among the majority
of the population while letting a privileged minority quite literally
get away with murder. Soysambu is a valuable, 30,000-hectare
property in the Rift Valley owned by the Delameres, a British
aristocratic family, and a major producer of meat, dairy, and
horticultural produce in Kenya. It also borders Lake Nakuru
National Park and hosts abundant populations of wild ungulates.
Carnivores are far less welcome on the property due to livestock.

In April 2005, Samson Ole Sisina, a KWS intelligence officer,
was investigating reports of game meat being traded under the
cover of meat from domestic stock. Several high-end Nairobi
restaurants at the time were serving game meat with very little
clarity provided on the sources thereof. Ole Sisina's investigations
led him to Soysambu farm where he confronted workers skinning
and quartering several impala and buffalo carcasses at the farm's
slaughterhouse. He identified himself as a KWS officer, drew his
firearm, and arrested the workers. The alarm, however, had been
raised, and Tom Cholmondeley, scion of the Delamere family,
rushed to the scene and promptly opened fire, killing Ole Sisina
instantly.

As expected, there was an immediate security response from
the KWS. Cholmondeley was arrested and prosecuted. After
lengthy deliberations, the attorney general simply entered a nolle
prosequi on behalf of the Government of Kenya, formally
terminating all legal proceedings against the accused. Effectively,
Cholmondeley only suffered a slap on the wrist and withdrawal of
his firearms license for the killing of a security officer on duty.
Those familiar with law enforcement in Kenya will know that the
killing of a security officer typically draws very harsh judicial
censure upon anyone who is lucky enough to reach a court of law.
However, most of those involved in such offences pay the ultimate
price extrajudicially.

Immediately following the incident, the private conservation
fraternity went into damage control mode, bandying about all sorts

of perceived justifications for Cholmondeley's reckless actions. These included the oft-repeated line of "There are robbers all over the place nowadays, and the KWS guy was not in uniform." This line of argument deliberately ignored the fact that undercover work is expressly defined by security officers' use of civilian attire. Furthermore, following his acquittal, Cholmondeley continued using firearms, which resulted in another shooting and arrest a couple of years later.

The reverse side of the myth that targets adulation for conservation work only at Caucasians is that it automatically excludes all whites from any association with poaching or wildlife crimes. This is a worldwide phenomenon that may have grown from the tone and content of early conservation literature and media. It is rarely acknowledged but hasn't escaped the notice of conservation scholars. Indeed, a definitive study on the history of conservation practices in Kenya by Edward Steinhart is tellingly entitled *Black Poachers, White Hunters*.

In reality, searches of wildlife crime records in Kenya over the last eighty years do not reveal any single occurrence of a white person being accused of or arrested for poaching. The earliest evidence of white settlers' involvement in wildlife crimes is a rather oblique reference from the chief game warden of Kenya in 1936 to motor poaching (the shooting of wildlife from motor vehicles) as a new challenge to wildlife conservation and management. Ownership of motor vehicles and guns in 1920s Kenya was very much the preserve of white people.

In more recent times, Kenya Wildlife Service intelligence officers organized a sting operation in 2013 in response to a spike in elephant poaching and ivory trafficking and netted Soila Saiyalel as she attempted to sell nineteen kilograms of ivory to an undercover KWS officer. This one arrest sent shock waves through the conservation fraternity, because Saiyalel is the deputy director of Amboseli Trust for Elephants, a well-known outfit that has been conducting research and monitoring on elephants in Amboseli since 1974. This project was started and is still directed by Dr.

Cynthia Moss, a world-renowned expert on the behaviour and ecology of African elephants.

Saiyalel, and her son Robert, were remanded into custody in March 2013, where they remained until March 2014 when they were both acquitted because of "tainted evidence." On March 14, 2014, the well-known conservation blogger Dr. Wolfgang H. Thome wrote, "It is heartening to see that for once Kenya's justice system worked and in fact stood up and threw out what was often described as an entirely frivolous case, smacking of an act of vengeance and vendetta." This is the same Kenyan justice system that has been roundly condemned (rightly so) for being too lenient on wildlife poaching and related crimes.

In the case, there were claims that Saiyalel was set up and the evidence against her and her son fabricated. Media reports, however, gave details of a car chase and the arrest of the suspects at Emali Town with nineteen kilograms of ivory in their car. The technical and legal details of the case are not available to us, but there is no doubt that there was some ivory being sold somewhere by somebody. Despite all the claims of a setup, there were no names furnished by the suspects of who framed them or were allegedly trading ivory. What is irrefutable here is that a deputy director of a world-renowned elephant conservation outfit was one of two names mentioned in what may or may not have been an ivory trafficking scandal. And there hasn't been any discernible effect of this scandal on the reputations of the Amboseli Trust for Elephants or its director.

Those acquainted with trends in wildlife crime know that 2013 was a year when Ivory trade and elephant poaching spiked in Kenya and was even discussed in the US congress and UK House of Lords. The slightest whiff of ambivalence towards wildlife crime, much less involvement therein, would be a guarantee of immediate and indelible opprobrium to the person perceived as guilty of this transgression. It took a full year for the Saiyalel case to reach its legal conclusion, and at no point during that time was the director's commitment to conservation questioned or any of the organization's conservation funding suspended. As of 2014, the world is not yet ready to even contemplate the possible involvement of white people from the West in any form of wildlife crime. This myth is very much alive in our society and remains as strong as ever.

We Are Watching You: The KWS Issues Stern Warning to Conservancies Over Poaching

Kenya Wildlife Service boss Mr. William Kibet Kiprono has accused some conservancies of collaborating with poachers to kill wild animals. Speaking during the wheelbarrow race at Hell's Gate National Park in Naivasha, Mr. Kiprono said he had a list of the conservancies and they risked being degazetted. "We have enough proof that some of the poachers are being aided by the so-called conservationists. In fact some even provide the poachers with the powerful weapons to kill wild animals," he added. The same conservationists then use photos of the dead rhinos and elephants to solicit funds globally to fight poaching in Kenya, he said.

Report by Joyce Kimani, *Daily Nation* July 28, 2014

Myths are known to persist and thrive under circumstances of limited knowledge or where an incomplete message is aired relentlessly. The whole world knows why wildlife crime (or any other form of organized crime) takes place: the profit motive. We also know very well who the beneficiaries of these illegal activities generally are: the poachers, traffickers, processors of wildlife goods, and corrupt enforcement officials at different levels. Close observation of the dynamics around this matter reveals that those involved with saving certain species are key beneficiaries as well.

In early 2013, there was a pregnant female elephant shot by poachers in northwestern Laikipia. The wounded animal escaped its assailants but later succumbed to its injuries on Suiyan Ranch where the staff duly removed the tusks and submitted the same to the KWS with a full report of the occurrence. During this activity, they also dissected the animal, revealing a fully formed foetus and took photographs of the scene. Space for Giants got hold of the rather macabre photos and promptly posted them on social media with an appeal for funds from donors to enable them to stop the slaughter. The response was swift and, admittedly, beyond what was expected by the authors of the post.

Firstly, there was the inflow of cash donations, which was described as overwhelming, although the amount wasn't specified. Other unexpected responses were a stream of vitriol (much of it steeped in racism) against Asians, who are perceived as providing the primary market for ivory, and the cruel savages who targeted this pregnant animal for profit and possible witchcraft purposes. Laikipia's reputation as a tourist destination was somewhat sullied by this post, but obviously nothing else mattered other than the finances that could be mobilized by posting such material online. Never mind that the poachers had nothing to do with the dissection of the elephant and dragging its unborn calf and entrails out into the open.

In this particular instance, the poachers did not get the tusks off this elephant, but if they did, it is unlikely they would have earned as much as Space for Giants did from posting the photos on their social media outlet. The odium generated by airing such material is regarded by practitioners as mere collateral damage, and the conservational end justifies the dishonest means.

Laikipia County in Central Kenya is home to all the Big Five species (elephants, buffalos, rhinos, leopards, and lions) and is the most important wildlife habitat in Kenya outside protected areas. A key component of this are the large, privately held landholdings therein. These were initially livestock ranches owned by the descendants of European settler families, but several of them have changed hands over the years for various reasons, including a decline in profits, the emigration of the owners, and a loss of interest in ranching and the lifestyle associated therewith. One thing, however, has remained constant. Whether the buyer is European, Kenyan or American, there is an unwritten rule: white-owned lands are always sold to white buyers.

Any possibility that this may be a coincidence is dispelled by the fact that all managers of the above lands are white. This kingdom, or any part thereof, is not supposed to fall into the hands of the *watu*. Many of these landowners have moved away from livestock production as a mainstay and are now wildlife conservancies with their primary aim stated as wildlife conservation. This move can be puzzling to the uninformed outsider, since the profitability of a conservancy is not immediately apparent. However, with the international connections these landowners have, conservation can be an extremely lucrative business, particularly when it is relentlessly marketed as a form of altruism. Literature and media are replete with apparently exceptional altruists who gave up careers in the corporate world, livestock ranching, academia, or the arts to save a species, a community, a national park, or a forest from imminent destruction.

This myth is so persistent that, even in this day and age of the global village, the mere act of a white European or American moving to live in Africa is seen as an amazing act of self-sacrifice. It is never quite the same for those of Asian- or African-American extraction. When this act is coupled with images of beautiful landscapes, acacia trees, sunsets, dead animals supposedly killed by poachers, you have a recipe that will loosen any Western purse strings. If you add images of the altruist with innocent young wild animals that would surely have died at the hands of savage people without the altruist's intervention, then you have hit the mother lode.

The financial rewards follow rapidly in the form of unbudgeted, unaccountable, and untaxed financial inflows from people all over the world moved by impending disaster and the amazing people who make the selfless sacrifice of leaving lives of luxury and security in the West to prevent it. These heroes are therefore not subject to the tedious routine of raising funds through proposals that state qualifications, work plans, budgets, and overall contributions to some official policy position or strategy. Donors are so enthralled with this myth that few care to imagine who these heroes were before they came to Africa or what they might have become in the West if they hadn't come to save Africa's wildlife from Africans. These questions might bring very sobering revelations indeed.

In the unfortunate event that any of these vaunted figures die out in the wild, regardless of the cause, their legend grows exponentially and is cemented. The conservation world so desperately needs them to die saving an innocent animal from the natives in order to append a tragic end to the romantic story of their lives. The late Joy Adamson, wife of George Adamson, is widely thought to have made the ultimate sacrifice for conservation, dying out in the bush in her beloved Shaba Reserve. The truth is much more mundane.

Joy Adamson was an extremely unpleasant person, mostly as an employer to her local staff, often threatening them with a gun for various reasons or to underscore her orders. She was stabbed to death by Peter Nakware Ekai simply because she refused to pay him his wages from the previous week. The measly wages paid to local labourers in rural Kenya and her refusal to do so are the clearest indication of Joy Adamson's character. It is highly unlikely that the amount owed to Ekai was any more than fifteen dollars. The effort to cover up any personality flaws was instant and universal among the media and her contemporaries. Dr. Cynthia Moss, a friend of Adamson's, was quoted as saying Joy had a "very strong personality, but would be highly unlikely to threaten or shoot at anyone with a gun." Dr. Perez Olindo, former director of the Kenya Government Game Department, said Adamson had "very strong opinions" and that she was very "unwilling to change."

Another example of eccentricity masquerading as altruism was the late Dian Fossey, who left everything behind to study and eventually work to save the mountain gorillas on Mount Visoke in Rwanda. The isolation of her camp and obvious closeness to the gorillas won her many admirers and created her legend. However, behind this façade hid a reclusive, insecure, and violent personality who severely mistreated even the few faithful employees willing to work for her in her cloistered and absolutist fiefdom. Her eccentricities included dabbling in witchcraft and violence to protect herself and her gorillas from poachers.

Her killer has never been found, but on the night of December 26, 1985, she died in her home from a single machete blow. Over $2,000, firearms, and other valuables in her house were left untouched, shutting the door on the shopworn robbery theory that is so often used to explain the homicides of foreigners living among impoverished Africans. The media asked no questions about her personality or her lifestyle. Everything written is about her lifelong struggle to save the mountain gorillas. The gorillas lived in Mount Visoke's forests long before Dian Fossey came and still survive nearly three decades after her passing. Would these animals have survived without our intervention? We will never know, because it is a question that is never truly asked. What matters is that her legend became canon.

The human condition needs and often cultivates romantic myths and legends around people who are unique in one way or another, and these remain important ingredients in the cultural fabric of any society. Conservation however is a practice that doesn't benefit from the myths created around the personalities therein. The most harmful effect of this Tarzan-and-Jane hero myth in African conservation is how it has diverted and created a hegemony on media attention and financial resources. It has taken money, attention, and effectiveness away from the many practitioners of all races who are truly committed to this cause. Ironically, those losing out on donor largesse are the ones who truly invest time, energy, and other resources to this cause, and those who train others to take the reins and eventually dismount from the horse to let this happen.

Scholars, practitioners, and observers of conservation in Kenya are respectively guilty of covering up and ignoring the history of human interactions with wildlife across the world. The

larger and potentially dangerous megafauna have always held a
special place in the human psyche through the ages. Lions for
example, have always been considered to be regal symbols of
bravery, power, and virility in various cultures. The different
manifestations of the lion's place in human thinking include the
traditional Maasai lion hunt as proof of bravery, the Lion of Judah
characterisation of Emperor Haile Selassie, and the prominent
place of lions on the Kenyan coat of arms. The spell cast by the
charisma of lions has spread far and wide, beyond the species'
natural range, into the circuses of ancient Rome and the royal
emblems of modern England. Other African wildlife was even used
for practical purposes in ancient Europe, with elephants playing a
prominent role in several Roman military campaigns.

With the benefit of this glance at history, it is easy to see why
mere images of George and Joy Adamson walking through the
African bush with *their* lions in tow cements their reputation as
conservation icons, regardless of whatever else they did (or didn't
do). It also makes it much easier to understand why images of
Dame Dr. Daphne Sheldrick hand-rearing elephant calves have
spawned an entire foundation and earned her several honours for
her part in saving the African elephant. It doesn't matter that over
the years she has received and spent many millions of dollars in this
endeavour, rescuing lost elephant calves and rearing them to
adulthood, an activity that doesn't constitute a contribution to the
survival of the species but absorbs money intended for true
elephant conservation.

The understanding and study of conservation in Kenya and
Africa as a whole is greatly retarded by the myths around it, but
there are some nuggets of truth that are beginning to emerge from
this blanket of misinformation. An example is the positive step that
the Kenya Wildlife Service has taken in erecting a memorial in
honour of sixty-one rangers who have been killed by poachers over
the years fighting wildlife crime. It is, however, a shame to the
organization and the country as a whole that it took us until
December 2011 to do so. The names inscribed on the monument

are the people who actually gave their lives for the cause of conservation. They never claimed to be altruists. They simply did the job they were trained and sworn to do with bravery and professionalism. Why they aren't well known and celebrated even by their compatriots is a question that conservationists can defer but never escape. There are many factors at play in their anonymity, but it is a fallacy to imagine their race isn't one of them.

It may yet not be on any visible horizon, but human society will be far better off when this myth is discarded and we are left with a firm understanding that conservation work is not altruism. Conservationists are people with the same material needs and foibles as everyone else. They don't do it for free. Any objective private or institutional donor should also embrace this understanding of conservation work. The reason why anyone would present a proposed work plan and budget running into the millions without a salary line is not because he is doing this work for free. It is because the structure of his operation entitles him to the entire some of money granted.

It is a startling anomaly that with the almost universal access to intellectual resources in the twenty-first century, conservation still largely fails to examine itself through the prism of human dimensions or sociology. Sociological analyses have bestowed significant progress on several other fields, including education, medicine, and economics. The resultant lack of progress in the human dimensions of the field of conservation has created space for the proliferation and advancement of the myths we struggle with in conservation practice to this day.

6 ~ The Prostitution/Tyranny of Science

Dr. Ogada and a colleague collaring a leopard. Conservation research in Kenya often uses animal handling and collaring as an escape from the human issues underlying Kenya's gravest conservation challenges (©Mordecai Ogada)

It is widely accepted that research is one of the key pillars of any successful wildlife management regime or conservation policy. The essence of this argument is the fact that conservation is the management of dynamic living systems and has to constantly adjust to new realities. Kenya is no exception to this rule but suffers from a deep schism between research output and management practice. As a result of extensive study, adventure, and coverage in print and electronic media, African wildlife has captured people's imagination worldwide. For similar reasons, Kenya is arguably the most sought after and romanticised platform of human-wildlife interaction in Africa. The country is extensively quoted and covered in artistic and scientific study. However, closer observation of these materials reveal very limited involvement of the indigenous populace in these interactions, be they peer reviewed publications, books, films, still photos, popular press articles, or lectures at international forums.

At first glance, this may seem like a new phenomenon based

in communication channels, but it is in fact a paradigm that has persisted since the days of the great hunting safari, when the African was a prop for photographs and almost as much part of the safari equipment as the gun, camera, or hunting knife. Old safari photographs show very clearly that the intellectual pursuit of wildlife, whether for study, photography, sport, or consumptive use, was a sphere in which the indigenous populations were very firmly denied agency.

Foreign domination of conservation science and direction in Kenya is still widely accepted as the norm. The Kenya Wildlife Service still pays lip service to science, and its conservation standing suffers as a result. This is a remnant of the institutional culture instilled by its founding director, Richard Leakey, who had an instinctive distrust of any science he couldn't immediately understand and discount. Given his lack of formal education, his tenure at inception was the death knell for most science within the institution. To cover up this obvious lacuna, he performed a quick window-dressing exercise by appointing the vocal and ambitious Dr. Paula Kahumbu as scientific advisor to the director, essentially a gatekeeper position.

This office was put in place as an effective shield to rebuff the heretics who felt that science could actually contribute to the mission of the KWS. Even after two decades, the staff of the KWS, who are styled as scientists, are simply stationed in offices with duties that are largely limited to clerical work for external researchers and periodic wildlife counts. They are also regular attendees at conservation conferences worldwide at which they never give presentations or contributions to the scientific programs, which is not surprising considering that 99 percent of them obtained their advanced degrees within the intellectual straitjacket that is the KWS, which essentially operates merely as one of Kenya's regimented security organs.

In theory, all foreign wildlife researchers in Kenya are supposed to go through a permitting process that includes the Kenya Wildlife Service and the National Council of Science and

Technology. Ostensibly, this is to ensure that the government is privy to all research proposals, processes, and findings by these scientists while in Kenya. The reality on the ground is that there are numerous foreign researchers and students studying and bioprospecting in Kenya on tourist visas that can be renewed every three months with a smile, a wink, or a quick nip across the border into Tanzania. Kenya only reacts with outrage when we find out about a microorganism discovered in a Rift Valley lake that has been used to produce a safe and effective organic bleach to replace sodium hypochlorite.

Nothing illustrates more starkly the inability of the KWS to participate intellectually in conservation than the robust and long-standing debate on conservation legislation and policies in Kenya. This is typified by the ten years it took to redraft the Wildlife (Conservation & Management) Act of 2013. The debate has been covert and overt through personal connections and media organs respectively, and the biggest bones of contention have been the status of conservation outside protected areas and consumptive use of wildlife. The KWS and its officers have been prominent by their silence about the legislation and policies that they are mandated to implement in Kenya. There has never been any media article or statement by the KWS conservation officers or scientists on conservation policy and legislation debates. These problems persist because, since the early twentieth century, local Kenyans have been relegated to the position of bystanders in conservation policy and practice.

The greatest concession to this status quo is the fact that the locals (most crucially the wildlife authorities) have accepted and embraced this position, thus handing the discourse on Kenya's most valuable resource to foreign profiteers in various guises. The term scientist is the most effective profiteering disguise, due to the implication of altruism that is wrongly associated with conservation science, which is deliberately held over from the days of the explorers, when venturing into the unknown or *dark* continent involved a high degree of self-sacrifice and extreme hardship.

It is worth noting that this romanticism and myth of sacrifice in regard to conservation does not extend to other fields of science; the world does not regard a prominent nuclear physicist or chemist as a self-sacrificing hero. This myth is relentlessly fed in word and deed by all interested parties. Mordecai Ogada has attended conferences during the freezing European and American winters held in high-end venues where heroes with six-figure grants and fellowships resolutely walked around and held court in dirty shorts, t-shirts, sandals, and unkempt beards. A prime example is Mike Fay, whose claim to fame is his much-vaunted Megatransect walk across Central Africa ending at Gabon's Atlantic coast in October 2000 over a year after he began.

Most readers of *National Geographic* cannot fathom how Fay survived in the jungle for so long, because they don't know about the regular air-drops of essential supplies. More knowledgeable wildlife biologists were enthralled at his reports of meeting forest elephants that "had never seen human beings,' never mind that he was being guided by locals who had been using this same forest for generations. As with Krapf, Livingstone, Rebmann, Stanley, and the others who had gone before, something known to local Africans was still considered new to science, new to the world. Western students, journalists, and junior scientists hold these adventurers in awe mixed with consternation at the apparent indifference of nonbelievers like Ogada. This legendary status is what profiteer scientists saving African wildlife aspire to, because once attained, they are above reproach, their names unlock funding, and their words direct policy.

At the 2007 Society for Conservation Biology Conference in Port Elizabeth, South Africa, Dr. Stuart Pimm, a world famous conservation biologist and professor of conservation biology at Duke University, gave a plenary speech that lamented the huge amount of conservation research that goes on in Africa, and contrasted it with the almost total absence of African scientists from the resultant literature. A stunned silence fell across the hall when Ogada asked whether this wasn't a result of foreign researchers struggling to maintain their relevance and funding streams.

Any close observer will notice that very little conservation research happens as a quest for solutions to conservation problems and involves very little local capacity building other than what is imposed by either funding or regulating agencies. Funding agencies are acutely aware that a research project performed by a local African scientist will cost a fraction of the cost as performed by a foreign expert, due to huge overheads, including the costs of airfare and numerous emoluments (none of which are ever referred to as salary or taxed by statutory authorities). This particular group's rule of thumb for survival is therefore the need to maintain a conservation crisis, or the perception thereof, and to maintain an intellectual hegemony of the issues at hand.

Where the involvement of locals is unavoidable, they are allocated a section of the data to analyse and write up for an academic degree. There is no intellectual input from local participants into the formulation of any research questions. And these academic bones are highly sought after by officers in statutory bodies like the KWS, because they confer degrees (and all the privileges that appertain thereto) without the responsibility of contributing to science or its transfer into policy and management. Kenya is now beginning to reap the bitter fruits of this complacency in the face of scientific dishonesty. This country's needs are still not addressed by the majority of ecological research being undertaken here.

Firstly, there are several challenges to wildlife conservation that are not based on wildlife crime. These include habitat fragmentation, habitat degradation, and invasive species. The Kenya Wildlife Service is unable to address these because the solutions aren't based in law enforcement machinery, and that is the limit of their capabilities. The scientists within the KWS who are tasked with addressing these matters are out of their depth due to scientific inactivity and tend to be otherwise occupied attending conferences and workshops. It is especially telling that twenty-five years after its establishment, the KWS still doesn't have a research laboratory or dedicated scientific facility; it has only a forensics lab.

In 1997, as a fresh zoology graduate, Ogada sought a research internship with the KWS and received the following response, "KWS is not a scientific organization, we do not need zoologists here—we only need wildlife management graduates from Moi University." The speaker was Dr. Wilbur Ottichilo, ironically then Deputy Director in charge of research. Discouraging as this response was at the time, it was also an assurance that in seeking to get into wildlife research, Ogada certainly wasn't entering a saturated field.

Then there are the incessant wars Kenya has to fight at the annual meetings of the International Convention on Trade in Endangered Species (CITES). Kenya, as a key beneficiary of the international ban on ivory trade, always seeks an extension thereof but consistently arrives to the convention with a delegation that has no scientific data or knowledge to back their position. What then follows is political horse-trading with other nations and their species and raucous shouting down of the proponents of ivory trade.

Granted, this strategy has served the delegation well in the past, but it is unsustainable in an educated world, and their successes are waning. This tactic is totally dependent on animal welfare lobby groups like the International Fund for Animal Welfare and the hue and cry raised by a number of individual activists who have the wherewithal to fund their own participation. The precarious nature of Kenya's position is always lost in the noisy victory celebrations by the huge delegation that often include the minister, ministry officials, KWS board members, and assorted relatives and friends of each of these groups. The victorious group returns home bearing various stuffed animals (including elephants) that are carried aloft and *vuvuzelas* that are blown in celebration. Victories (such as the 2011 verdict) obtained in this manner are typically short lived. For example, during the Conference of Parties in 2013 in Bangkok, CITES allowed limited trade in ivory stockpiles, and the impact on elephant conservation is plain for all to see.

And the least visible (but potentially most harmful) result of dishonesty in the scientific sector is the resultant diversion of resources and attention to what in dialogues with the lay community is euphemistically called *pure* (as opposed to *applied*) research. In reality, this is the narrowing of a field of study down to a level where an individual or small group can realistically hold a monopoly over its practice and any resources dedicated thereto. At the turn of the century, this was down to the study and conservation of individual species.

This approach is weak among conservation principles, because no species exists in isolation, but nevertheless, the conservation world and its financiers embraced (among others) Cynthia Moss, Iain Douglas-Hamilton, and Joyce Poole as authorities on elephants, Craig Packer and Bruce Patterson as authorities on lions, and Hans Kruuk and Laurence Frank as authorities on hyenas. A number of these individuals moved to higher levels of study, looking at habitat variables and the human dimensions of conserving their said species, but the majority stayed firmly in the *authority* comfort zone that guaranteed continuous funding and publications in increasingly narrow niches.

As with every rule, exceptions to this modus operandi do exist among the expatriate conservation ecologists in Kenya. The two examples that stand out are Drs. Laurence Frank and Truman Young of the University of California Berkeley and the University of California Davis respectively. Dr. Frank is a pioneer in the behavioural physiology of spotted hyenas who moved into the study of carnivore ecology and conflicts with humans, particularly in the arena of livestock depredation. This progression moved his focus beyond the ecology of carnivores into the study of human attitudes and behaviour around carnivores. This focus on communities led Dr. Frank towards addressing the real challenges that face wildlife managers in the conservation of carnivores and the sustenance of human livelihoods around their habitats.

The remarkable Lion Guardians program with Maasai *morans* in southeastern Kenya is Dr. Frank's brainchild and a telling demonstration of what can be achieved with an inclusive approach. In conservation literature, this particular initiative has been hailed as a great innovation and a major breakthrough in human-wildlife conflict mitigation. The real accomplishment here, however, is Frank's understanding that there must be existing conservation ethics in communities that have lived with wildlife for thousands of years, in spite of their perceived poverty and supposed Hobbesian existence. This radical departure from the well-trodden conservation path is as much an indictment of the wider conservation fraternity as it is a credit to Dr. Frank.

Conservation, by definition, is a long term objective, and consequently, any conservation work that does not have environmental, social, and economic sustainability built into it is fundamentally flawed. The cornerstone of any exogenous conservation initiative is therefore the development of indigenous local capacity to carry it forward. Sadly, this approach is the exception rather than the norm among the vast number of foreign conservation biologists plying their trade in Kenya. Many excuses are bandied about to explain this shortcoming, including resource limitations, difficulty in finding capable local students, and others. The real aim however, is to maintain the conservation problem, the funding streams, the relevance of the individual in perpetuity. This can be done differently, as evidenced by the efforts of Dr. Truman Young.

In an ecological research tenure spanning nearly two decades based at the Mpala Research Center in Laikipia County, Dr. Young has authored over sixty publications and supervised four Kenyan PhDs and three MSc projects among a much larger complement of foreign students. The significance of these numbers lies in the total scientific output, which is approximately 320 publications by over 1,000 different authors and a local authorship component of approximately 5 percent of that number. Dr. Young is still a highly relevant, much published and quoted research scientist, proving that loss of relevance is not a valid fear for avoiding to embrace indigenous scientific interest and talent.

It is worth noting that the number of local PhDs from Mpala not involved with Dr. Young's projects is two, meaning that this one scientist has trained twice as much local expertise as all others combined. These figures are a source of great concern when one considers that this institution is arguably the premier wildlife and ecosystems research facility in Kenya. In addition, the National Museums of Kenya and Kenya Wildlife Service both pose as board members, dutifully attending meetings but not offering any apparent intellectual input into the management of the center

A particularly telling example of the difficulties facing the evolution and democratization of conservation research and practice in Kenya is the case of the Hirola antelope (*Damaliscus hunteri*). This is a critically endangered species that is endemic to a limited range in eastern Kenya. The Northern Rangelands Trust, through its community conservancies, seeks to enclose the remaining few hundred individuals inside a predator-proof enclosure, ostensibly to ensure the survival of the species. Apparently, the NRT, with all the field research expertise at its disposal, concluded that predation was the cause of this species' precariously low population.

From an ecological standpoint, there are several drawbacks to this proposed solution, mainly because the reasons for the low Hirola population are far from being well understood. For instance, if it is related to parasites or disease, basic ecology states that restriction of the remaining animals will only exacerbate the effects thereof. Furthermore, if the problem is habitat loss or fragmentation, the deliberate limitation of their remaining habitat cannot be helpful in any way. From a different perspective, much of eastern Kenya has been identified as a key remnant habitat of two wide-ranging and critically endangered species, the cheetah and the African wild dog (*Lycaon pictus*); the latter thought by some to be a key culprit in the decline of Hirola. The Kenya Wildlife Service published a ten-year conservation and management plan for these species, which specifically identified habitat loss and fragmentation as a key threat. How then did the same KWS authorise a nonstate agency to effectively privatise a species and expressly fragment crucial wildlife habitat? The answer lies in the status of Ian Craig, the founder of the NRT and a member of the KWS board at the time of this development.

Craig's position on the board proved more powerful than the published species strategies and the ecological knowledge of the described scientists at the KWS. A lay person might wonder what the purpose of such a project is, other than the apparently altruistic pursuit of noble conservation objectives. To the initiated, however, critically endangered and endemic species are known to be magnets for conservation funding, and enclosing the Hirola in this manner is an effective net around that money. More evidence of this intention is evident in Craig's reaction to the conservation work on Hirola antelopes being done by Abdullahi Hussein Ali, a very promising young Kenyan conservation biologist who also happens to be from the part of Kenya concerned with the Hirola.

Ali has been looking at indigenous knowledge of the Hirola that exists in the local community, habitat variables, and telemetry studies for his PhD studies at the University of Wyoming. He is also involving the county government in his proposal to establish a Hirola reserve. The NRT has offered resistance to Ali's work, and Ian Craig, in particular, has made a declaration that the project will fail. As things stand, Ali's project is proceeding successfully, and his work has been recognised through various awards from international foundations and the Garissa County government.

By all estimates, the Kenya Wildlife Service should be the leader or coordinator of wildlife research in Kenya, but thus far it has failed dismally in this mandate. The low regard in which it's founding director, Richard Leakey, held science as a conservation tool still persists decades after his departure. There have since been attempts to form ad hoc committees into which external experts were brought to assist with the management of particular species or taxa, including elephants, rhinos, Grevy's zebras, and carnivores.

The KWS staff who liaise with committees are, however, unable to synthesize the local expertise at their disposal into coherent management actions for these species, even where there are well-written management plans. As a result, they are still vulnerable to manipulation on the basis of personal whims that have little basis in the practice of science or wildlife conservation.

The KWS carnivore management committee is one that is regularly exposed to these personal agendas, some of which simply expose high levels of ignorance, but others pose serious policy questions. In 2000, there was an ongoing program to bait and kill lions in Aberdare National Park, purportedly because they were depleting the population of the highly endangered mountain bongo. Tens of lions were killed inside a protected area by the agency tasked with conserving Kenya's wildlife for reasons that did not involve conflict with humans.

More recently in 2008, there was a request put to the KWS to cull 50 percent of the hyenas in Aberdare National Park because a visitor was very upset to see a pack of hyenas killing a rhino calf and concluded that this was cruel and detrimental to rhino conservation. Fortunately, this particular request was subjected to technical scientific scrutiny and later found to have no merit, not least because the actual hyena population in the Aberdares National Park wasn't known. To the casual observer, the technical examination would indicate the KWS moving towards science based wildlife management, but the truth is more mundane. This request, lacking in any conservation merit, was only entertained because the visitor behind it was a member of the KWS board.

The most recent manifestation of this institutional weakness within the KWS was a "species strategies harmonization" meeting held at Lewa Wildlife Conservancy in October 2012. The quorum was made up of nineteen stakeholders, which included eight KWS staff, among them a senior scientist and a deputy director. The basic agenda was whether to allow the culling of lions in the Lewa and Ol-Pejeta conservancies because of their seeming preference for Grevy's zebras and black rhino calves as prey, causing further decline of these endangered species. The Grevy's zebra species management plan was being put forward as a basis for this request, and its proponents already had in place a plan of action for culling. There were some protestations from KWS officers about this carnivore management strategy and the need to conserve carnivores, but the culling agenda was well prepared and was holding sway.

In his submission on behalf of the carnivore management committee, Ogada stated three main points: Firstly, the fact that wildlife species do not exist in isolation, and conservation is the maintenance of life and death cycles but not of one species at the expense of another. Secondly, Ogada quoted the Lotka-Volterra model of predator-prey dynamics that essentially states that an indigenous predator cannot hunt a prey species to extinction before dying out itself, due to its own energy needs. Lastly, Ogada stated that permitting the culling of lions would be a precursor to sport hunting, because the argument would immediately be raised over why we should wastefully cull lions for free when there are people ready to pay tens of thousands of dollars to hunt one and others ready and capable of managing the hunts. This final point was raised as a worst case scenario, but the deafening silence and fidgeting that followed the remarks indicated that it didn't represent the profanation Ogada held this scenario to be.

The final decision on the culling request was deferred until more meetings were held and the relevant literature was properly reviewed. In the end, the Ol-Pejeta and Lewa lions' lease on life was extended as the proponents of the plan restrategized. In a private conversation later, one of the KWS officers thanked Ogada for his contribution, saying that they couldn't say those things because of the presence of Ian Craig (of the NRT), who was one of the authors of the request and a KWS board member. A look at the quorum reveals that there were ten representatives of the culling school of thought, including eight representatives of the KWS who were unable to think or speak independently on the issue. Out of nineteen participants, Ogada was the only independent voice who was not beholden to any viewpoint other than science.

There are many other instances of this institutional weakness, including the licensing of the late Mutula Kilonzo, a former Minister of Education, to keep pet lions and cheetahs at his ranch in Machakos in express violation of the KWS's own management strategies for these species while the media and public celebrated him as a conservationist. It is informative that months after the Kilonzo died, his descendants could not take good care of the animals. This is a snapshot of our conservation policy process in Kenya today: both the owners of the resource and those holding it in trust sitting on their hands while vested interests and profiteers have their way.

Exogenous conservation initiatives are generally not interested in solutions simply because solutions will render them redundant and divert funding to other newly deserving causes and projects. This chapter has detailed the nature of the cutthroat competition for territory (geographical, financial, and taxonomic) and ownership of the conservation sector and its manifestations. What then are the net effects of these tendencies on conservation itself? A major cost incurred by this sector is the movement of significant financial resources from pressing national and international conservation issues to scientific minutiae. This term could raise questions by its apparent reference to science that is of little use or application to real world problems.

It is a widely accepted paradigm that biological sciences are all practical and real, but where there are practical problems that need to be addressed, biologists can be guilty of unacceptable esotericism. An example of this is the touted ground-breaking study conducted in southern Kenya by Prof. Karen McComb and Dr. Graeme Shannon from the University of Sussex who found that elephants can distinguish between Maasai and Kamba voices and displayed symptoms of agitation when they heard Maasai voices. This study certainly doesn't stand up to technical examination if it presumes to reduce mature African languages to the level of voices.

Even if these findings were technically sound, what good is such knowledge in the face of the grave conservation and wildlife crimes facing the African elephant? The current levels of poaching, ivory trafficking, habitat loss, and conflict with humans really doesn't give us the luxury of diverting research funds to the pursuit of such minutiae. A significant part of this problem is the alacrity with which local scientists jump onto bandwagons, put down their names as collaborators, and assist with permitting and fieldwork just to get per diem allowances and occasional mentions in the acknowledgement sections of the resultant publications or theses.

Science is (or should be) the basis for all the major strides made in human development in the sectors of health, nutrition, engineering, and so forth. Conservation practice in Africa has sadly made itself an exception to this rule, and the evidence is clear. In this case, science has been and still is the vehicle through which foreign interests have established a hegemony over Kenya's environment and wildlife. And Kenya as a country is squarely to blame for this state of affairs, having no locally based or conceived wildlife and ecosystems research agenda in any of our institutions or universities.

As a nation, Kenya encourages and awards drama, music, beauty, entrepreneurship, broadcasting, arts, and other pursuits but not science. We also participate in a contradiction in that we criticize, question, and analyze these other pursuits but do not extend the same scrutiny to science, thereby denying good science the support it needs and excusing spurious science from the opprobrium it deserves. Science, like all other human pursuits, has evolved to become a means to progress, profit, and other human ends. Kenya's most precious resource is its environment and the wildlife therein. Kenya needs to embrace conservation science to meet its conservation and economic needs. In the current scenario, Kenya (its needs, people, and institutions) will remain spectators or mere pawns in the allegory of a dark, unspoiled continent and the outside interests that seek to bring in the light as they exploit her body and her gifts.

7 ~ Conservation: A Thickly-Veiled Scheme to Grab Africa's Resources?

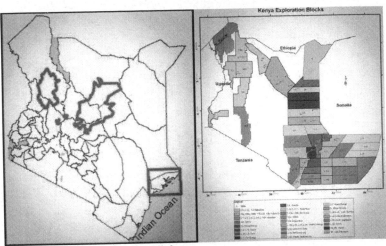

Map © David Ouma (Adapted from
http://www.nrt-kenya.org/regions

**Food for thought: Territory covered by the Northern Rangelands
Trust conservancies, and a map showing Kenya's oil exploration
blocks. (©NRT, ©National Oil Corporation of Kenya)**

The authors' work in conservation journalism and conservation
biology has resulted in close interaction with many schemes,
cliques of conservation personalities, and different situations that
nourished a belief that the entire conservation agenda in Africa is a
thickly veiled push to grab and hold on to some of the continent's
defining resources. Through long and close interaction with this
deceit, the authors found ample evidence that many of the
overglorified personalities in conservation, some of whom enjoy
global adulation for saving this or that species, are little more than
knighted super con men and women who, in different
circumstances, would be in jail (or worse) for what could be
categorized as elevated forms of treason. But this might not
happen owing to a long-running grand deception in which the
victims are made to believe that the crimes are committed for their
own good and that it pays to remain hungry and eat the crumbs as
they allow others to fatten from overfeeding on their behalf.

In our view, conservationism assumes that government sanction, the bribery of boreholes and classrooms, the willful blindness of the media, and a cheering global audience on incessant lookout for heroes and heroines to worship will forever hide this reality. Steeped in self-inflicted contradictions and enjoying the immense wealth emanating from a form of resource-access apartheid that stretches back more than a hundred years, key players in African conservation have continued to delude themselves that it might take all eternity for natives to realise that an exaggerated love for animals is camouflage for more sinister schemes. For the schemers, the big agenda has been, and continues to be, to continue to champion conservation and to use different forms of bribery to keep the natives unaware under the guise of promoting the preservation of much of Africa's unexploited natural potential.

In Kenya, the latest fad has been the creation of wildlife conservancies of immense size, which is done under the very eyes of clandestine outfits and officialdom that are either irreparably blind or too willing to play along. Kenyan law has been progressively changed to ensure legal protection of these conservancies, while the United Nations Educational, Scientific, and Cultural Organization (UNESCO) is increasingly being called upon to declare such areas as world heritage sites. As a signatory to the World Heritage Convention, Kenya, and the rest of Africa, can only play the unwitting victim of the deceit by complying once the UNESCO plays ball. Following this, the UNESCO has already declared Lewa Downs as part world heritage site and is expected to assign this status to many more ranches in the county. But lately, Kenya has shown some uncharacteristic belligerence. By starting grandiose infrastructure projects such as the 2.5 trillion Kenyan shilling ($2.5 billion) Lamu Port–Southern Sudan–Ethiopia Transport, a corridor that is planned to connect Kenya and neighbouring states, Kenya has lately not been a cooperative lap dog.

A veritable army of foreign conservation biologists, ecologists, and so-called conservationists have lent their names and research to this mushrooming conservancy fad in return for a share of the considerable largesse tied up in consultancy. This frittering away of donor funds is often carried out under the guise of research consultancies, which are essentially unaccountable and unverifiable services rendered to a host of organizations by people who claim various scientific or experience-based qualifications. These services include expertise in fields like grazing coordination and rangeland rehabilitation, which can hardly be taught by an outsider to communities who have practiced pastoralism for millennia. In the rangeland rehabilitation arena, a never-spoken truth is that the degradation of rangelands and apparent increase in livestock density is the direct result of creating exclusion zones for tourism in conservancies while banishing the owners of these lands to the rocky peripheries of their birthright. To silence and convince critics and doubting Thomases, strange arithmetic is applied with an aim of showing just how much communities need such schemes. Following this, the Northern Rangelands Trust, for example, can now boast openly of commanding some six million acres (or 44,000 square kilometers) of real estate in upper eastern, northern, and coastal Kenya.

The initial concept of the community-owned wildlife conservancy was an idea not totally lacking in merit. The overarching aim was to create coherent structures and demarcate areas within which communities could formally manage their communally owned lands for the sake of conserving wildlife therein. Recent developments, however, have revealed fundamental (if not fatal) flaws in the original thinking on conservancies. The hurried and externally driven creation of such bodies as group ranch committees and grazing committees was based mainly on the assumption that prior to the conservancy being created, no order or established channel of dialogue among communities was needed. This notion forms the basis of the deliberate destabilizing and dismantling of traditional order and norms that have existed for centuries. The timing of this move, however, was perfect in terms of current conservational thinking among practitioners and, crucially, donors.

The central theme and message coming out of the 2003 World Conservation Union's World Parks Congress held in Durban was benefits beyond boundaries (i.e., ensuring the flow of revenues and other nonmonetary benefits of parks to the communities that share habitats with wildlife outside the parks). This came after several years of growing criticism of the fortress conservation model that laid emphasis on the fencing and patrol of parks to protect wildlife. The model that proposed establishment of conservancies outside protected areas therefore gained immediate currency and caught the eye of donors, as well as statutory agencies like the Kenya Wildlife Service, which was keen to gain more habitat for wildlife and secure reservoir wildlife populations that could augment those in parks via wildlife corridors.

The leading exponent of the conservancies model in Kenya is the NRT, formed in 2004 in the heady community conservation atmosphere that pervaded the worldwide conservation sector immediately following the 2003 World Parks Congress. Land is probably the most important component of any terrestrial conservation plan, and this new paradigm was based on what were euphemistically described as nonprotected areas. This definition is fundamentally flawed in that it presumes to describe entire swathes of land in terms of stating what it is *not*. The more truthful term would have been to describe the move as conservation of wildlife in community lands. However, this description would necessarily have entailed the inclusion of the relevant communities, their livelihoods, and their aspirations in conservation plans. With this carefully laid out and presented plan to secure the future of wildlife in these vast lands while civilizing and structuring the communities living there, money rapidly flowed in from private and institutional donors. To the parties interested in the use of these lands and resources, the communities' needs and goals were details so inconvenient as to render them practically impossible to address. Thus began the mass disenfranchisement of communities in the name of conservation, and the rest is history.

But the push for more land in the form of conservancies is not a one-off affair. Neither did it happen out of the blue. It is part of long-running schemes in which well-positioned conservationists (either as individuals, groups, or NGOs) have positioned themselves to reap big as the world continues to sing their praises. One of the most audacious of these schemes was when some in this lot attempted to grab all moneymaking ventures of the KWS in 2004. This was well into the era when the grabbing of resources in Africa and other parts of the developing world was euphemistically labeled privatization. This was also long after the World Bank demanded poor countries to open up their key sectors to be devoured by multi-national corporations and other private profiteers in an inhumane and horrific plot dubbed structural adjustment programmes.

John Mbaria was then working with *The EastAfrican*, a regional weekly read in Kenya, Uganda, Rwanda, and Tanzania. Through bold, no-holds-barred, and consistent coverage of developments in the conservation field, Mbaria had developed a sizeable following and attracted significant loathing, particularly from some prominent personalities in conservation cliques. Many went out of their way to steer his pen in directions that were more agreeable; others raised obnoxious tirades on whatever he wrote. But he had also developed a strong rapport with his sources—who are so valued in journalism. One day in August 2004, one of Mbaria's sources happened by the *Nation* newsroom, where John also plied his journalistic efforts, looking for him. The man was carrying a document detailing how British businessmen, led by one Andrew Hind, had ganged up with Kenyan conservationists and several key people in government to partially buy out the KWS by putting under their control all the KWS's moneymaking ventures.

To contextualize this audacity, there is a need to appreciate that, as the successor agency to the Wildlife Conservation and Management Department, into the hands of the KWS was accorded the control and management of about 8 percent of Kenya's territory in 1989. Within this slice of real estate are sixty national parks and reserves, as well as 125 wildlife stations outside protected areas. Although only a few of the parks generate revenue, by 2004, the KWS was bringing in an annual revenue of 800 million Kenyan shillings. But the wildlife agency was not just running on its own finances. Indeed, from the very word go, the KWS was primed to largely run on donor funding. Using his substantial international reputation, Richard Leakey had managed to secure significant funding from the World Bank under the five-year Protected Area Wildlife Service (PAWS) programme. He partly used the cash in a grand reconstruction programme that included putting up a modern complex at the KWS head office, building up the wildlife agency's fleet of vehicles, and sprucing its image. Doing this was easy for Leakey; he drew from personal charisma and a go-getting attitude.

But Leakey also came up with and embraced unsustainable measures that worsened the fortunes of the KWS, as well as Kenya's wildlife sector. For instance, he ordered the payment of hefty salaries to a select number of senior staff, to the chagrin of long-serving wardens and rangers. These elevated salaries continued even after the PAWS programme came to an end. At the same time, Leakey had used some of the donor funding to buy aircrafts and vehicles without setting in motion a discernible kitty for maintenance, which meant using much of the KWS's dwindling revenue base to maintain them. Unbeknown to a praise-singing world, Leakey began a long tenure of mismanagement that fed into what was seen as a deliberate scheme to weaken the KWS. This left the wildlife agency on its knees, which encouraged some of the donors to call the shots as one director after another went on begging missions. But they could not outdo Leakey at this game. The man had almost personalized the KWS's relationship with donors to an extent that when he left, his replacement, David Western, was unable to draw to the agency the same amount of funding. Things moved from bad to worse, forcing Western to use the land belonging to the KWS's training school in Naivasha to secure funding from the Kenya Commercial Bank.

The wildlife body was also reeling from a confused policy and legal milieu that had not been corrected ever since it was formed in 1989. For instance, the law stated that all wildlife—from beetles to elephants and everything in between—belonged to the people of Kenya and was held in trust by the government. It failed to recognise, as a fundamental principle, that not all wildlife was held in lands belonging to the state. This had allowed for confused interpretations of the law while the wildlife policy enacted in 1975 had become obsolete, so far as reality and the socioeconomic dynamics prevalent in the 1980s and 1990s were concerned.

This confused legal and policy framework had given a cabal of mostly white game ranchers, who possess vast swathes of wilderness, justification to influence the KWS's operations. Many were not satisfied with photographic tourism and kept churning out reports that disputed the value of some of the ranches under this form of use. They also organised copious monthly talks, through the East African Wildlife Society, that were mainly presided over by those who shared prohunting sentiments. Constantly, the cabal also nagged the KWS, seeking to be allowed to engage in consumptive utilisation—a long-held euphemism for sport hunting. Besides hosting wildlife and keeping livestock, many of the ranchers were operating on new and old money (acquired through massive robbery and exploitation of Kenyans during the colonial period) and had retreated into wildlife conservation, where they have used their money and clout within Kenyan society to influence how laws and policies that might be injurious to their interests are enacted.

In the 1990s and well into the 2000s, these white game ranchers maintained a long jeremiad on how the wildlife they host on their ranches had surpassed their carrying capacity and was not only destroying crops but also competing with and killing livestock, yet they were not getting much in terms of benefits. They wanted to be allowed to kill (or *cull*) some of the animals and commercialise related services and products. Their target was to sell hunting safaris to rich clients from Europe and America, who are known to spare no coin when purchasing the pleasure of shooting animals for fun. They also targeted highly lucrative markets for the skins and hides in South Africa and envisaged juicy slices of game meat would fetch top dollar in expensive restaurants in Nairobi, Mombasa, and elsewhere.

Leakey, who had continued to pose as a champion of nonconsumptive wildlife use, proved that he was not averse to the interests of the white ranchers. He yielded to their demand when the KWS allowed them to begin killing game under the Wildlife Pilot Cropping Project, a wildlife cropping programme that started in 1991 and remained an *experiment* for more than twelve years. The scheme involved assigning an annual shooting quota to ranchers who could prove that they hosted more animals than their lands could carry. Such proof came from poorly paid KWS personnel who would be dispatched to the ranches to conduct wet and dry season animal counts and later come up with a formula for assigning the quotas. Most of the white ranchers ended up with quotas that enabled them to kill hundreds of zebras, antelopes, and buffaloes. They reaped immense profits from selling hunting safaris to rich clients from the US and the Middle East and offloading the skins and meat.

As detailed in the report *Evaluation of the Wildlife Pilot Cropping Project*, the entire experiment was deliberately designed to be faulty from the word go. It was not only poorly planned but plagued by massive abuse, with many of the ranchers manipulating the statistics so they could get larger quotas even as others killed more animals than provided in their quotas. Written by Dr. Jim Kairu of Tasha Bioservices Ltd., the report also says that landowners continued to pressure the government to lift the ban on sport hunting put in place in 1977. The stated objectives of the pilot project included the reduction in wildlife-related costs, the development of markets that would allow consumptive use of wildlife to be economically viable, and the assessment of the feasibility of continuing and expanding the project. Animal killing activities were to be overseen by the KWS and implemented by ranchers, croppers, and game meat outlets. It was only meant to run for five years in Samburu, Laikipia, Nakuru, Machakos, Kajiado, and Lamu County before being evaluated to determine whether the project was to be continued and expanded. However, it became so lucrative that it was allowed to continue for thirteen years with no evaluation or study until the eleventh year of operation.

To make the project work, the KWS was supposed to train croppers and marksmen in the initial phase. But this did not happen. Instead, the mostly white ranchers, especially those in Machakos and Laikipia County, established their own operational regulations without adequate involvement of the KWS, and thereby untrained hunters often injured animals that ended up dying slowly from their wounds. And furthermore, when experts at Tasha Bioservices conducted the evaluation of the pilot project in 2001, they established that, besides leading to a marked decline in wildlife populations in areas where cropping was taking place, only a few small-scale white ranchers were awarded user rights, which caused conflicts, especially where large-scale landowners had little interaction with neighbouring communities.

The project was also plagued by sheer discrimination, in that native communities who also hosted vast numbers of wildlife were initially not considered in the scheme and only received extremely low quotas after much hue and cry. And often they would end up selling their quotas to white ranchers anyway, largely because they did not have access to the market and were not given licenses to bear firearms. To the discerning observer, the practice of sport hunting under the guise of cropping was very obvious because the croppers were selling raw zebra hides to processors in southern Africa at approximately thirty-five dollars per hide, a pittance that could never cover the cost of procuring the same.

All this did not escape the notice of communities on whose lands some of this cropping was taking place, which resulted in increased poaching (particularly for bush meat) in nonprotected areas, along with communities voicing protest that the landowners were effectively involved in legalized poaching while common citizens were arrested for snaring dik-diks. Also, as observed by Salisha Chandra, the coordinator of Kenyans United Against Poaching, the methods used in the project to count animals were not species-specific and yielded unreliable results. There were disagreements as to who needed to undertake each animal census, what methods needed to be employed, and whether verification was necessary; indeed, the allocation of quotas was not grounded on a sound scientific approach. Instead, censuses and quotas were done and allocated on an individual ranch basis as opposed to an ecosystems approach, which would have been more appropriate. The quota allocation was itself done through open cheating and corruption. The gravy train came to a standstill in 2003 when media reports covered these abuses, forcing the environment minister, the late Newton Kulundu, to discontinue the scheme.

In part, this scenario prevailed before the advent of the plot to take over all the KWS's moneymaking ventures in 2004. Andrew Hind, the man behind the takeover scheme, was a British national who then owned the Wildlife Café Group in London. Hind, it later emerged, was invited by Collin Church, a soft-speaking, elderly businessman who then headed the KWS Board, to write a deceptive concept paper, "The Commercialization of the Kenya Wildlife Service: Concept Document." The KWS's revenues are generated from different moneymaking ventures that the schemers targeted to wrest from the state and hand over to a private company. Hind was also a director of Bill Jordan's Wildlife Defense Fund and secretly schemed with others in Kenya for a month before the document he drafted became public. "The proposed deal to turn the KWS into a commercial company was allegedly made without Cabinet approval," and for that matter without the knowledge of most of the KWS board, wrote Biketi Kikechi of the *East African Standard*. Oscar Obonyo of the *Daily Nation* wrote, "Enumerating his wildlife conservation activities, which include donating 50 percent of the profits of his restaurant, The Wildlife Café, and sponsoring several projects in Kenya and other countries, Mr. Hind maintained that he is a conservationist who believes that wildlife can raise revenue from tourism without having its life threatened." Obonyo continued, "His idea is the introduction of commercial policies which make money from tourism, merchandise sales, memberships, hotels, and safari camps." It was apparent that Hind was a typical charlatan altruist who believed that his business model was what Kenya desperately needed to ensure continued survival of her wildlife species and populations. Nowhere in his paper did he ever mention how he, and his company, were to benefit from the privatization. Everything he and his cohorts had planned to do was purportedly for the good of Kenya and its wildlife.

One year earlier, the same clique had mooted a grand plan to hand over some of Kenya's national parks to a Dutch billionaire, Paul van Vlissingen. Vlissingen was an interesting character. When he died, *The Guardian* newspaper described him as a "Dutch entrepreneur and philanthropist . . . one of the wealthiest men in Europe and a progressive landowner in Britain who devoted much of his personal fortune to conservation projects in Africa." Born near Utrecht during the German wartime occupation of the Netherlands, Vlissingen refused medical treatment after been diagnosed with pancreatic cancer and went on to manage the family firm, SHV Food & Energy Group. In 1974, at the age of thirty-three, Vlissingen joined SHV's board and oversaw its diversification and rapid growth at a time when the world was reeling from an oil crisis. Soon, the company became one of the largest in the Netherlands, employing more people than most of its contemporaries. The growth also raised Vlissingen's fortune; the man was worth some £1 billion by the time the cancer ended his life. With all this money, he turned himself into what *The Guardian* proclaimed an "expert shot" and acquired the Conholt Park estate near Andover, Hampshire, where he traded in the pleasure-killing of wildlife through what was hailed as a "model of conservation."

Vlissingen wished to be seen as a philanthropist with an urge to help African communities but was accused of significant proapartheid investments in South Africa in the 1980s. To redeem his image, he founded the African Parks Foundation after meeting the late Nelson Mandela in 1998, who told the Dutch billionaire that local people's social needs must override wildlife conservation. Vlissingen appears to have been startled by Mandela's advice into establishing what was hailed in the West as a welcome outfit that managed nature parks in seven African countries and was "seeking to balance the interests of wildlife and tourism with those of local people." Though, Vlissingen did not see anything wrong with pursuing his animal-killing pastime while still spending millions from his vast fortune to prevent Africans from engaging in hunting for the pot. He embarked on what the *Daily Telegraph* described as "a remarkable personal crusade to transform failing game reserves in Africa." He saw this as part of giving something back, reversing the damage wrought on the environment by Africans. To his credit, however, Vlissingen eventually admitted that part of the damage done to various African ecosystems had been caused by his own family's business.

In a typical fashion adopted by conservation do-gooders from the West, the eccentric billionaire pumped €25 million into a scheme partially aimed at giving money directly to villagers previously prosecuted for killing animals to deter them from more killing in Zambia, while he himself continued to relish in killing animals for fun. The cash was also used to relaunch the Marakele Park in South Africa, which was opened by Mandela and the avowed sport hunter the late Prince Bernhard of the Netherlands, as a public-private partnership and to run Majete and Nech Sar parks in Malawi and Ethiopia respectively. Later, the BBC reported on June 16, 2003, that after being emboldened by his interaction with Mandela, Vlissingen's company, now renamed African Parks Management and Finance Company, planned to take over a string of national parks throughout Africa, starting with parks in Zambia, Malawi, Uganda, Kenya, and Mozambique. Mandela was not the only one to support the scheme; the BBC reported that the US State Department and the World Bank had warmed up to it on the belief that this was the only way game reserves would be saved from neglect and local poachers who hunted them bare. "The state could bring in expertise, scientists, and animals from other national parks and land, and I could bring in management expertise and the drive to make it go," Vlissingen told the BBC.

But Vlissingen's self-protestation to excellent management acumen did not assuage critics. For instance, after he acquired concessions to run two of Zambia's national parks, Sioma Ngwezi and Liiuwa Plains, a Zambian radical legislator, Sakwiba Sikota, was so incensed that he declared the deal an ill-conceived theft: "This is an ill-conceived agreement, it borders on theft and plunder of the resources of the people of Barotseland and should be thrown out. No company should be given absolute rights over the people's natural resources unless it is owned 100 percent by the people of

Barotseland themselves." The Zambian lawyer-legislator went on to demand that Zambian officials behind the deal be exposed and investigated. Terming the deal a "modern day recolonisation and exploitation of Zambians," Sikota's choicest criticism landed on Vlissingen: "He . . . probably got his riches by exploiting Africa's natural resources." Sikota later referred to the deal as "the crime of the century."

In the South African province of Limpopo, Vlissingen hatched another deal to partner with the South Africa National Parks (SANParks) for the purpose of consolidating the original Marakele Park situated near Waterberg Mountain in western Limpopo, the Welgeyonden private game reserve, and his own 20,000-hectare Marakele contractual park into an enlarged 110,000-hectare Marakele National Park. As reported then by the South Africa-based *Citizen Newspaper*, the scheme involved getting his own company, Marakele (Pty) Ltd., to fence in, rehabilitate, and introduce new wildlife species. For allowing part of South Africa's natural heritage to be run by a private profiteer, SANParks was to get a mere 4 percent of the turnover from commercial operations and 50 percent of the park's entrance fees.

Vlissingen, who earlier had been buying out farms in the area at double their market price, mooted plans of bringing in private investors to build exclusive, upmarket lodges in the reserve and to provide accommodations that would have been affordable to local visitors. In the well-crafted deal, the Dutch tycoon looked forward to selling the land he had bought, which constituted his Marakele contractual park, to the South African government at, as he told *Citizen Newspaper*, "the price he had paid for it plus inflation" (i.e., a profit). And he did not blush when he later said, "I am not looking for wealth. I want to do something that is good for the planet and for the people." Further, supporters of the scheme loudly proclaimed that it raised revenues for SANParks and brought employment and other goodies for the local people.

As all this was taking place, the interests of the local communities—who were described by some of the Western media as "stubbornly poor"—were totally disregarded. For example, like their counterparts in other countries of Africa, the interests of the people of Barotseland, Zambia, featured nowhere as Vlissingen took over their natural heritage. Media outlets in the West outdid themselves to paint the Barotse, through politically correct jargon and phrases, as fiends who needed Vlissingen's millions so those outlets could look the other way as Vlissingen's company hogged further millions from an enterprise that owed its revenue base to traditional African conservation ethics. As he predicted total collapse of the wildlife populations across the continent, the billionaire was a strange contradiction; although he killed many animals elsewhere across the continent, he still believed that he was what God and nature intended to liberate Africans from a self-inflicted myopia and self-destruction. What is not surprising, however, is the fact that his continued exploitation of African natural resources for tourism purposes found the prompt approval of the US State Department, the World Bank, and Nelson Mandela.

To give private profiteers like Vlissingen legal and policy backing, the IUCN-inspired World Parks Congress held in Durban, South Africa, in September of 2003 sought to whitewash private sector involvement in wildlife-based businesses by asking governments, NGOs, and indigenous communities to "remove the obstacles to, and enhance the opportunities for, public–private–community partnerships in protected area management and funding to ensure sustained conservation of biodiversity, natural values and cultural heritage." Governments were specifically implored to develop appropriate legal, administrative, and financial instruments and to implement new partnership arrangements for the benefit of both protected areas and their private sector partners. Although some words were thrown in to provide for what were termed *mechanisms* for a more effective, equitable, and efficient distribution of returns to protected areas from emerging environmental services markets, the motivation was to ensure that private companies were able to zero in on, and profit from, what indigenous communities had so well preserved for centuries.

Vlissingen was to advance his glaringly audacious business exploits to Kenya when he hosted top officials from the Kenya Wildlife Service in South Africa in June, 2003, around the time the KWS was operating at a substantial loss and was heavily dependent upon foreign grants, which also jeopardized national control of wildlife conservation policy and practice. The closest that the KWS came to attaining self-sufficiency was when Nehemiah Rotich became the head in July, 1999, and reduced its budget deficit from 588 million Kenyan shillings to 30 million Kenyan shillings. But the cartels controlling the wildlife body would have none of it; Rotich was fired under unexplained circumstances in December, 2001. When he was later interviewed by Nixon Ng'ang'a of the *East African Standard* (now *The Standard*), Rotich complained of a series of transactions that were mooted and actualized (by the cartels) to "weaken the KWS financially." He charged that the KWS was deliberately run down so that "privatization appears to be the only viable option." But he was optimistic that if properly managed, the wildlife agency could develop all of the viable economic opportunities envisioned by Hind and others without surrendering any control of natural resources and without subjecting Kenyan wildlife to consumptive use.

The KWS then (and even today) was at the mercy of wildlife cartels that are mainly composed of white game ranchers, key personalities working for big-buck international NGOs, top businessmen with tourist concerns, senior government officials, and foreign nationals (mainly from Britain) whose main goal has been to influence Kenyan conservation policy and how the wildlife agency is run. Although each of these groups has specific drives, in general, their aim has been to ensure that policy and the KWS's operations favour their fund-raising and commercial interests. Indeed, when Rotich was axed from the KWS, the cartels influenced the appointment of Michael Karathi Wamithi as the KWS director in a move that surprised and angered many observers in almost equal measure. But to hand it to him, the petite, soft spoken Wamithi was ethical in his dealings before and during his short stint at the KWS. He was a career game warden who had served for fourteen years in the KWS where he rose through the ranks from an assistant warden to assistant director in charge of intelligence. In his time at the KWS, Wamithi worked in the Nairobi, Tsavo West, and Amboseli National Parks, Wajir District, and Mombasa and was reputed to have come up with a list of security hotspots within Kenya's parks and reserves and for having designed and developed effective intelligence procedures and policies in the wildlife agency.

Indeed, Wamithi was more a victim of shenanigans than a participator. He also seemed a tad too naïve to accept going along with such schemes. He most likely did not have full knowledge of what he was getting himself into. His appointment was some short months after millions of Kenyans had done away with KANUism and Moism—mongrels of ideology that had little to do with political dogma; they were merely about the sanctioned robbery, corruption, deceit, and survival antics of Daniel Moi, the former president of Kenya, and his small clique of top government officials and wheeler-dealers.

Away from this group was a viciously efficient conservation fraternity that operated in a less crude manner but nevertheless had captured portions of the wildlife sector for its own interests and had strangulated any moves to make it work for the interests of the country and the long-term survival of wildlife. The fraternity was godfathered by Charles Njonjo, a former Attorney General and incessant praise-singing practitioner of English mannerisms. Njonjo was appointed chairman of the KWS after being rehabilitated from the cold by Moi following long years of political oblivion—a consequence of his alleged role in schemes to overthrow the latter. He was later pardoned by Moi after going through a long-drawn inquiry that drew widespread public interest.

Besides Njonjo was Leakey, whose cunning and sheer audacity backed by the right skin pigmentation and famous lineage ushered him from one senior position to the next, ultimately ending with the undeserved position of the head of Kenya's civil service. Richard Leakey and Charles Njonjo headed the KWS's board of Trustees in the early 2000s. On his part, Leakey had earlier served twice as the head of the KWS, attaining, as stated earlier, a mixed record of performance that was praised and castigated in almost equal measure. But to his credit, Leakey managed to convince an adoring global fan base that his two terms at the KWS were full of achievements. But though the man was associated with ridding Kenya of a poaching menace that had threatened to wipe out all the country's jumbos, rhinos, and other signature species, no one has ever truly put this claim to objective scrutiny. In books and media reports, adoring journalists—even those who knew better—grossly overlooked his weaknesses as a manager and transgressions as a conservationist as they outdid themselves to accord him an indelible conservation myth that has survived virtually unscathed.

Ultimately, Njonjo and Leakey were the men Wamithi was to work under. Although the law required both to head a nonexecutive KWS board, the two appeared to have had a lot of time on their hands, which they used to micromanage affairs at the wildlife body. It was while they headed the KWS board that the plan to hand over some national parks in Kenya to Vlissingen was mooted. However, the role that the two played in the sterile scheme was not so direct, as neither of them traveled to South Africa to meet Vlissingen. Instead it was Wamithi, Dr. Paula Kahumbu, and other top KWS officials who made the trip.

In hindsight, the involvement of Kahumbu, who at the time worked as an assistant director in charge of National Parks and Reserves, in the scheme was interesting because she all along put out an image of the infallible campaigner for the welfare of animals, especially elephants. This has partly been through her noisy Hands Off Our Elephants campaign, through which she has continuously lambasted all and sundry—particularly anyone who does not subscribe to her version of what is the right conservation agenda for Kenya.

Wamithi, in particular, was to later suffer the brunt of his unwitting participation in Vlissingen's scheme when he was fired by then Environment Minister, the late Newton Kulundu, in May 2003. When doing so, Kulundu justified it by stating that Wamithi was fired for undermining the government's conservation efforts. This ended Wamithi's stint at the KWS. Wamithi later went back to the International Fund for Animal Welfare, where he served as the head of its elephant programme before moving on to the Kenya Wildlife Trust.

Following these major changes in the KWS's leadership, Kahumbu was also caught in the storm. The former scientific advisor to Leakey was coached and mentored by the man himself and had run the Colobus Trust while conducting her Ph.D. research on elephants in the Shimba Hills. She resigned from the KWS in June 2003. Soon after, She was embraced by the Lafarge East Africa Company, a cement-making company that appointed her the general manager of its subsidiary, Lafarge Eco Systems. In her often self-publicized claim, Kahumbu asserts that she willingly left the KWS because she could not agree with the conservation direction it was taking. But this is not entirely true, because together with other senior staff who enjoyed huge perks at the KWS, the Leakey protégé found the going tough in the early 2000s, especially when the KWS started a process of restructuring.

This restructuring targeted officers with privileged salaries who had continued to earn elevated perks even after the Leakey-negotiated, World Bank–funded Protected Area Wildlife Service project became defunct. On the authority of Leakey and Njonjo, the KWS had also retained by contract certain retirees, whose pay continued to drain the wildlife agency's dwindled resources. What escaped media attention then was, as public servants, Kahumbu and Wamithi had crossed the red line by flying to South Africa to negotiate with Vlissingen on how the latter could take over Kenya's national parks without knowledge or express authority of higher powers, and especially the Kenyan cabinet. It is instructive that when he sacked Wamithi, Kulundu said the government was caught unawares by the plan to privatise the parks.

This saga draws to mind how much Kenya's wildlife conservation sector has been dominated by only a few people. It also shows that this group has been willing to ignore Kenya's law, the government, and the people as it once attempted to handover the country's parks to foreign profiteers. This is impunity of the highest order, which in different circumstances would have resulted in conviction and possible imprisonment. It is also a clear demonstration of the powers wielded by this group, because even after the scandal came into the public limelight, none of those involved were charged. And, in any case, some have continued to dominate conservation activities and dialogue in Kenya.

Manufactured Coincidences

Coincidences, as defined by the Merriam-Webster Dictionary, are situations in which events happen at the same time in a way that is not planned or expected. But coincidences can be manufactured. In certain cases, there is a fine line between deliberate game plans and coincidences. The world is full of schemes that keep some in a perpetual state of opulence, even as the vast majority in society squeezes out very little from what, in a different epoch, ought to be part of the commons, or resources jointly owned and used by people occupying a given geographical area. This, as Garrett Hardin says, is the "tragedy of the commons." Hardin says:

> Everyone tries to reap the greatest benefit from a given resource. But as the demand for the resource overwhelms the supply, anyone who consumes an additional unit directly harms others who, at some point, find that they can no longer enjoy the benefits.

174

To ensure that no one upsets the apple cart, every effort made to shine the spotlight on manufactured coincidences, and hence open the eyes of the victims, is promptly dismissed as conspiracy theory, with those behind the effort labeled conspiracy theorists. This penchant to dismiss links between the past and the present, as the following section shows, is what has regrettably met anyone brazen enough to connect historical dots with current scenarios as far as the grand conservation program in Africa is concerned. And once the situation is painted in such a manner, an almost impenetrable conceptual lid is put on the truth. But some truths, as a former US State Secretary, Donald Rumsfeld, once said are "known knowns." Truthful truths cannot *just* be wished away.

At a time when there is a renewed scramble for Africa's resources, we find enough justification to conclude that the exaggerated love for Africa's wilderness and what is contained therein, as well as the overconcentration of the global conservation cult on the continent, is a thickly veiled scheme to hold on to the continent's defining resources. We base this on several seemingly unrelated historical incidences and developments. For instance, while addressing the media in 2003, the then Russian Ambassador to Kenya intimated that Russia knew what mineral resources the country's subsoil has as early as the late 1940s. It later emerged that in that decade, under contract from the British, Russian geologists had done explorative studies in the country and had mapped out what minerals Kenya has and where. Incidentally, this was around the same time the British colonial administration embarked on the declaration and gazettement of game parks and game reserves, starting with the Nairobi National Park in 1946. From this, one can only ask, could there be credence to the muted claims and suspicions that most so-called wildlife protected areas are host to much of Kenya's mineral wealth?

And how have the British secured or attempted to preserve such resources for future use? Another manufactured coincidence is that since independence, and earlier, there has always been remnants (and inheritors) of the colonial order within and adjacent to Kenya's protected areas. These people are the so-called Kenyans of British descent who have made national parks or areas around national parks (i.e., wildlife dispersal areas, nonprotected areas, or wildlife migratory corridors) their permanent homes. Carefully, this lot has ensured that no suspicion of their true intentions is ever made by forming NGOs and coming up with research and species-specific wildlife conservation projects that are widely supported locally and internationally. For instance, Nairobi National Park is manned by Dr. Daphne Sheldrick, an elderly mother figure who runs an orphaned elephant rehabilitation project; at different points, the Tsavo national parks have been under Peter Jenkins, David Sheldrick, Bill Woodley (before he was transferred to man Mount Kenya and Aberdares), and Woodley's son, Bongo, who worked for seventeen years as a senior warden at the KWS; the Samburu National Reserve has Iain Douglas-Hamilton, who runs the Save The Elephant NGO; and Amboseli has Dr. Cynthia Moss, who runs the Amboseli Trust for Elephants NGO. Further, for close to fifty years, Richard Leakey has operated a field school close to Lake Turkana and the Sibiloi National Park. Some of these so-called altruistic conservationists and researchers have been in the wilderness for more than forty years studying a single animal species. The official narrative (which has been repeated again and again) is that these inheritors of the colonial order have been helping Kenya to conserve endangered wildlife species besides encouraging African communities to appreciate animals through community conservation schemes and the bribery of boreholes.

But that is half the story. The untold half is that the British have all along known exactly what minerals Kenya has and where they are located; they are also suspected to have spirited out relevant geological maps shortly before Kenya's independence in 1963, thus denying the incoming government this vital information. Secretly and through several schemes, the British have managed to continue preserving these minerals more than half a century after Britain handed over the management of the country to a trusted group of Kenyans. They have also managed to hide this fact from most Kenyans. For instance, one interesting anecdote related to this is that for decades school children throughout Kenya were taught in geography lessons that the country does not have minerals apart from soda ash in Lake Magadi and diatomite in the Kariandusi area in Nakuru County. This ensured that at their most impressionable age, millions of Kenyans have ingested and propagated the lie that their country has little or no mineral wealth.

Another coincidence is that during the colonial period, the British authorities declared upper eastern and northern Kenya (or the Northern Frontier District) no-go-zones and required visitors to acquire a special permit to enter there. This worked well, because since Kenya attained partial self-rule, African bureaucrats have shown marked disinterest in directing public investments to develop these areas; neither do they appear to want to know what else, apart from copious numbers of livestock, vast plains, and incessant conflict, exist there. Kenya's leadership has long acquiesced to the status quo in these areas, even as a sprinkling of Kenyans of British descent have gone on to perpetually monitor what happens to the country's rangelands (i.e., what happens to the minerals and other resources preserved therein). The scheme appears to have worked until Mwai Kibaki became president and led Kenyans in believing that the country's fortunes would change for the better if it established economic links with China and opened up these areas for development. This led to a significant development of infrastructure by Chinese companies.

One interesting offshoot of Kenya's economic dance with the East has been that shortly after the Chinese began sniffing around the rangelands, all of a sudden Kenya started discovering minerals, such as titanium ore and rare earth in Kwale County, coal deposits in the Mui Basin of Kitui County, iron ore in Isiolo County, Meru County, and other places, oil reserves in Turkana County and the Lake Victoria basin, and more. The lessons taught to millions of Kenyan children about a dearth of minerals in the country have now been thrown to history's dustbin. Interestingly too, nearly all the companies that have either been making these discoveries or continue to prospect come from the West (i.e., Britain, Australia, Canada, and to a lesser extent, American companies or their affiliates and subsidiaries). Although this is seen as an attempt to lock out China from venturing into Kenya's mineral sector, it is also a testimony to the fact that the British (both in the UK and the diaspora) have all along had, and kept secret, useful information on Kenya's mineral wealth.

Is it by coincidence that many of the mineral discoveries made in recent years in Kenya were in areas that have long been monitored by the same inheritors of the colonial order? For instance, oil was discovered by the British company Tullow Oil in Turkana County decades after Leakey made Turkana his base for paleontology research and where his outfit, the Turkana Basin Institute (TBI), has continually hosted foreign researchers in a place that is far from official oversight and the eyes of intelligence outfits. Together with his wife, Meave, and other fossil hunters, Leakey operated in Koobi Fora, located to the east of Lake Turkana, and later launched the TBI after joining hands with the US-based Stony Brook University in 2005. What is interesting about the operations of the TBI is that it hosts mainly foreign scientists and students and gives them, what it terms on its website, the opportunity to understand not only "how wildlife has greatly impacted the landscape" but also "a geological way of thinking, learning about the Sedimentary Geology and Geochronology of the Turkana Basin." This has raised suspicions that relevant scientists had been prospecting for oil long before Tullow Oil made public its oil discoveries there.

As if to ascertain the involvement of Leakey and the TBI in Kenya's budding oil sector, Tullow Oil states in some of its annual reports that it has partnered with the National Museums of Kenya, as well as the TBI, in the implementation of its socioeconomic projects for the Turkana community. The authors have also seen minutes of a stakeholders' meeting held in February 2014 attended by Leakey, who is mentioned as the founder of the TBI, and Alex Mutiso, who represented Tullow and others. The meeting was called to discuss concerns for the well-being of the environment in Turkana County following Tullow's oil prospecting activities there. Interestingly though, the TBI describes itself as a privately funded, nonprofit institution that has "carried out works in Turkana for the last fifty years and [has] a lot of archaeological, paleontological and geological information of the areas east and west of Lake Turkana." The inclusion of "geological information" in the statement appears to authenticate claims that the visiting scientists that TBI hosts have been acquiring geological data that must have been useful to Tullow Oil.

Interestingly too, the National Museums of Kenya have been manned for decades either by the Leakey clan (Leakey was once the managing director of the National Museums, while Meave and their daughter have held senior positions there) or by trusted cronies, including Mzalendo Kibunja and Dr. Paula Kahumbu, who was appointed to chair its board in 2016. With this in mind, and bearing in mind information contained in the minutes, several questions that Kenyans have raised over time regarding Leakey's connection to oil prospecting in Kenya and how wildlife conservation has been used to hoodwink Kenyans as to the true intention of the conservationists now have answers.

Some questions raised in the past include: Could it be that Leakey has been hosting mineral explorers at the TBI rather than fossil hunters? What is the true relationship between Leakey and Tullow Oil? What has been Leakey's true role in the discovery of oil in Turkana? Could it be true that oil and natural gas were discovered in Kenya in the late 1940s (when prospecting began) and, all along, Kenyans were hoodwinked with the story that discoveries made then were not of commercial value? Could it be that certain personalities were given the role by Britain of ensuring that other nations (such as China) did not gain access to such minerals? Is it by coincidence that so many of recently discovered mineral deposits are in areas now controlled by the redoubtable Northern Rangelands Trust, which was founded by the proprietor of the Lewa Wildlife Conservancy, Ian Craig? Today, the NRT claims to have brought some 44,000 square kilometers under wildlife conservation flying the banners of private and community conservancies. However, its attempt to start conservancies in Turkana suffered a major setback when the Turkana County government declared *illegal* six community conservancies in January 2016. Established by the NRT, these six conservancies were partially funded by Tullow Oil, which came into the picture in October 2015 after signing a five-year agreement with the NRT. Once again, this demonstrates the symbiotic connection between wildlife conservation and oil prospecting in Kenya.

Further questions have been asked on why schemes that initially appeared innocent and of benefit to local people in Kenya's drylands later turned out to be nightmares. One saga that comes to the fore is the relationship between the secret scheme put in place by the British to preserve Kenya's mineral wealth and the introduction of *Prosopis juliflora* (Mathenge) in most of Kenya's drylands. Known locally as Mathenge (after the official from the Kenya Forestry Research Institute who was directly involved in its propagation), it is an invasive tree species that has ravaged much of the country's rangelands. It was introduced to Kenya from Australia in the late 1970s and early 1980s by the Kenya Forestry Research Institute and the Food and Agricultural Organization with funding from the Australian government. Incidentally, at the time the Australians (mainly the British diaspora) were funding the project, they were also grappling with how to eradicate it in their own country. But years after it was introduced, it started colonizing vast tracts of land in Baringo, Tana River, Garissa, Turkana, and other counties. For instance, in the Ng'ambo area and other parts of Baringo County, the species literary displaced a large number of pastoralists and destroyed their livelihoods long before Cummins Co-generation Kenya Ltd. came in to set up a power plant in the Marigat area that was set to use Mathenge to generate power through gasification. (The company has temporarily suspended operation following serious disagreements with the local Ilchamus community.)

As a reaction to the havoc Mathenge has caused on their livelihoods, members of the Ilchamus community (or Njemps) took legal action against the government, seeking to compel the state to eradicate the invasive plant. To prove their case, they took a toothless goat to court, claiming that goats lose their teeth after consuming the plant's sugary pods. They also provided evidence of people who had lost limbs after being pricked by Mathenge thorns. But as the Mathenge saga unfolded, the question that still begs an answer is: What was the true motive behind the introduction of this noxious plant in areas that are suspected to have much of Kenya's mineral wealth? Can we believe without question that, as purported, its propagation was merely meant to prevent the spread of the desert into Kenya's drylands?

Other coincidences and relationships that need to be looked into include whether there is a link between the long-running inter-ethnic conflicts in much of the drylands of Kenya and the rising incidence of terrorism on the one hand and the desire to preserve mineral wealth for use by foreigners on the other. One question that requires immediate answer is how Kenya will ever retain its territorial integrity, peace, and national security against the backdrop of foreign companies that have been wantonly licensed to control nearly all of the forty-six Kenyan oil blocks (both onshore and offshore) that cover an area of over 400,000 square kilometers. Only two blocks were licensed to the National Oil Company of Kenya, which has since leased one to a Canadian company. And a coinciding issue that might eventually become a thorny national security matter is how the interests (i.e., ownership) of communities inhabiting lands within the oil blocks, some of whom have been duped to believe they are involved in wildlife conservation through community conservancies, will be catered to once the oil begins flowing through a soon-to-be constructed pipeline.

It might be unfathomable for most adorers of Kenya's top conservationists to imagine that some of the biggest names in conservation could be involved in ulterior schemes that occasionally so offend natives and native institutions to a point of resolving to kick them out of the wilderness. Usually, when this happens, the almost saintly image of the relevant personalities is temporarily shattered. But because they hold immense ability to contain the damage, the saints are able to ensure that such transgressions by the natives are either watered down or do not reach the eyes and ears of the Western public. But even when the truth is quite glaring, most people in the West seem too steeped in the conservation cult to even consider looking at facts as they are, and have been.

For instance, Dr. Iain Douglas-Hamilton is a man who has painstakingly and over long years worked to ensure that his larger-than-life research personality remains unscathed within Africa's conservation circles and beyond. Born on August 16, 1942, the bespectacled, ageing elephant researcher has crafted the envious image of a serious scientist, an academic who has consistently studied jumbos for more than forty years. To put a living claim to his experience and expertise, the founder of the Save the Elephant NGO has written books (some with his wife, Oria Rocco), made several films on his work, and ensured that the right eyes and ears listen to the numerous talks he has given for different universities, private foundations, and zoological societies all over the West. As if to complement this, different sections of the media in the West have written and featured many aspects of his life and work in numerous excessively positive stories for several decades. In the process, the world of donors has come calling (including one of Hollywood's most famous actors, Leonardo DiCaprio) with millions of dollars in donations. He has received numerous accolades from many organizations who consider him one of the world's foremost authorities on African elephants, as well as from the Queen of England, who inducted him into the Most Excellent Order of the British Empire in 1993, as well as naming him a Commander of the Most Excellent Order of the British Empire in 2015, for so-called services to wildlife conservation and work with elephants. It is out of this international recognition that he was invited in 2012 by the US Senate's Foreign Affairs Committee to give testimony on the link between poaching and terrorism in Africa.

According to Ian Parker's book *What I Tell You Three Times Is True: Conservation, Ivory, History and Politics*, Douglas-Hamilton's first career was managing a security company in London. In Kenya, he finally found an abode in the wilds of Samburu where he honed and sharpened his expertise on the behavioural traits of jumbos. Decades later, he appeared to have decided that the now defunct Samburu County Council (that granted him permission to study elephants within Samburu County) would not mind if he were to convert a temporary research campsite into what came to be the Elephant Watch Tented Camp, a commercial tourist facility situated along the Ewaso Nyiro River. However, Douglas-Hamilton was in for a rude shock in mid–May 2007 when the county council decided to kick him out of the county for going against an agreement he made with the local authority to promote the Samburu National Reserve through his publication, on the Internet and through local and international media.

This created substantial heat and excitement within Kenya's conservation circles, especially after the county council accused Douglas-Hamilton of joining a well-oiled campaign to block the construction of new tourist facilities in the Samburu National Reserve. As John Mbaria was to find out, the letter cancelling Douglas-Hamilton's agreement with the local authority was written by Daniel L. Leleruk, who then acted as the county clerk. Leleruk ordered Save the Elephants to leave Samburu in three weeks. Douglas-Hamilton later confirmed that he had actually talked against the planned tourist development in the reserve but denied he had issued a malicious statement. "All I did was to make a presentation on the implications of [new] tourism developments in Samburu during a joint meeting with the National Environment Management Authority," he said in an interview with Mbaria.

It emerged that, together with other players in the local tourism sector, Douglas-Hamilton was against the construction of a number of tourism facilities in the reserve by two local companies, Ukarimu Ltd. and Miiba Miingi Ltd., even after the they had been given a nod by the Samburu County Council and the National Environmental Management Authority. The renowned researcher believed that the addition of 413 beds (bringing the total bed capacity in the reserve to 751) through these facilities would worsen the environment of the reserve and threaten its ecological integrity. "The degradation [of the reserve] from further developments would not be sustainable," he said, adding that the places where they were to be located were already "congested," besides being places with the highest density of wildlife. This was the agreeable part of the narrative.

But as it later emerged, Douglas-Hamilton's push to lock out other investors might have been informed by a need to reduce competition to his family's commercial interests in the Samburu National Reserve. The county council alluded to this when it claimed that Douglas-Hamilton was, after all, an interested party in the reserve's tourism activities. Leleruk said that by denouncing the new developments, Douglas-Hamilton was actually trying to protect his tourism business: "Although Dr. Douglas-Hamilton's main preoccupation is elephant research, his wife, Oria Douglas-Hamilton, runs the Elephant Watch Safaris, which is located in the Samburu National Reserve." The company had then posted online promotional materials that stated that the exclusive, high-cost facility charged between 21,000 Kenyan shillings ($300) and 40,600 Kenyan shillings ($580) per person per night. Douglas-Hamilton could not deny that his family had commercial interests in the reserve: "Yes, my wife runs the camp . . . it is true, but I am a scientist and would never compromise my scientific work for business considerations." However, information posted on the camp's website then alluded to the fact that some of the activities of the two outfits were intertwined.

The story could have been seen as one more attempt by the ungrateful hoi-polloi to throw some dirt on the illustrious career and impeccable image of Douglas-Hamilton. But the episode was evidently part of a bigger scheme in which conservationists-cum-investors had ganged up with NGOs and other groups to instigate legal changes in Kenya that could preserve the status quo in the rangelands and deny any meaningful development there (especially by competing concerns). Douglas-Hamilton was to expose himself and his cohorts when he stated that the basis for his opposition to the relevant investments in Samburu had to do with the fact that the new investors had not complied with the 1999 Environmental Management & Coordination Act. But he forgot one slight detail, that his wife's outfit had also not conducted an environmental audit as required by the same law.

This evidence came to the fore when a team from the NEMA headed by then Director General Dr. Muusya Mwinzi conducted fact-finding missions during which they met with Douglas-Hamilton and made site visits on April 18, 2007, and April 19, 2007, in Isiolo and Samburu counties. It was also made clear that Douglas-Hamilton's anti-investment sentiments were part of a long-running scheme by the inheritors of the colonial order to frustrate the emergence of any business that might threaten their own interests in their vast slices of Kenya's wilderness. The group had previously held its own meeting on February 22, 2007, under the auspices of the Ecotourism Society of Kenya and the Kenya Tourist Federation and had invited the African Wildlife Foundation for purposes of coming up with objections that could effectively persuade the NEMA to cancel the Environmental Impact Assessment licenses it had issued to Ukarimu Ltd. and Miiba Miingi Ltd., the local companies that planned new investments in Samburu. They hung on to the argument that the construction of the proposed properties would pose irreversible environmental damage to the reserve. They also argued that the construction of the new lodges was against the general management plan for Samburu that was prepared in 2004 by the AWF and which ruled out new developments in the reserve proper.

The take on this saga is that it is a typical case of a well-funded NGO working hand-in-glove with established tourism businesses and a renowned elephant researcher to frustrate the emergence of economic ventures that would have meant more meaningful benefits to locals through income generation and employment than the bribery of boreholes, cattle dips, and classrooms so favoured by conservationists. As the saga unfolded and evidence on the business operations of the Douglas-Hamiltons adduced, it became clear that some altruistic conservationists are so blinded by their antiprogress schemes that they even go on to forget that they themselves might have broken the same laws that they ask others to obey.

The whole incident also demonstrates how the unwitting enactment of new laws has been working against Africa's best interests. Like other countries, Kenya passed the EMCA law at a time when the country needed to expand most sectors to absorb an ever-increasing number of youths seeking employment, raise investments, earn foreign exchange, and alleviate poverty. But as the above episode so clearly demonstrates, emerging investors are frustrated by a whole series of legal and policy do's and don'ts. What is most intriguing is how authorities have so far maintained silence as those enjoying a disproportionate pie of wildlife-based tourism gang up with foreigners, foreign-funded conservation NGOs, activists, and members of the academy to harp on the environmental consequences of ushering in progress in Kenya's drylands. Most often, these groups end up winning, because many of their members are influential personalities, able to craftily silence dissenting voices during the process of passing laws that are injurious to national interests. This lot is also greatly equipped with both old and new money, which enables them to consistently and painstakingly work for their own interests, as the vast majority of Kenyans sleep or are too busy being poor.

In light of the arguments presented in this chapter, the external (nonconservationist) observer might be prompted to ask, are Kenya's statutory bodies and processes secure from the interests of these modern day, land-based buccaneers? Recent activities in the wildlife sector are instructive: In February, 2015, there were public consultations on regulations to do with conservancies. The process (ostensibly led by the KWS) was funded by The Nature Conservancy, the power behind the Northern Rangeland Trust. As a result, the Kenya Wildlife Conservancies Association (KCWA) was formed to lobby for the interests of communities and is led by a very capable community conservation practitioner, Dickson Kaelo. However, the KCWA is now funded by the TNC. On the other hand, the community conservancies program at the KWS was built from scratch by one of the most capable assistant directors at the KWS, Munira Bashir. She is still very much a leader in this sector, but now works as Kenya's director for the TNC.

EPILOGUE

There is no doubt that Kenya's conservation sector has long been mired in a miasma of conflicting needs, weak policies, corruption, greed, and outright lies used to cover up all these ills. What is there to be gained by writing and speaking so extensively about them? The most immediate gain is catharsis, the appreciation and acknowledgement of the way Kenya as a country has pursued the practice of conservation, the way in which we have put aside our interests, culture, vast tracts of land, finances, and needs as a nation to conserve our heritage in the manner in which we think outsiders would like to partake of it.

The difficulty of writing about current issues in a field where one is active makes it harder to step back every now and again and make sure one is still writing about the forest and not the tree one is sitting under. The need for serious introspection has never been greater than it is right now for Kenya's conservation sector, and we as a people must be prepared to ask ourselves the difficult questions. As a nation, we have reached a critical stage in how we relate with each other and the natural fabric that sustains our lives. A break from the past, as evidenced by reforms in most sectors, is imminent and desirable. Although we are yet to attain a unity of purpose, although past bad governance habits and corruption have prevailed to a significant extent, we are trudging on, travelling along our own chosen path, following the promulgation of the Kenya 2010 Constitution. This has ushered in a noisy clamour for all manner of freedoms, albeit empty-belly freedoms. But for some reason, reforms have largely escaped the wildlife conservation sector where both of the authors have spent much of our working lives.

Why is it so difficult for us to divest ourselves of the ambivalence and bystander attitude that outsiders have so carefully cultivated in our people since they landed on our shores over a century ago? There is no doubt whatsoever that Africa's greatest asset, after its people, is the sheer abundance and diversity of natural life with which this continent is endowed. It is also worth mentioning the resilience of these ecosystems and their constituent societies, because they have survived over 400 years of wanton destruction and plunder at the hands and technological implements brought in by outsiders. If we invested even a modicum of

186

intellectual energy in thinking about our natural heritage, we would realize that what remains of our natural heritage exists because of our stewardship and not because those who spent over four centuries destroying it have now spent four decades trying to conserve it. With this in mind, it would be a very small step for us to claim ownership of this heritage and conserve it, as we do everything that is precious to us. *Precious* in the precolonial African context is a term that implies the intrinsic value of a resource and has very little, if any, monetary connotation about it. The wildlife and forests that exist now outside the protected areas do not exist because they had monetary value to the local inhabitants. They were kept intact by the beliefs locals had in their sanctity, the reluctance of locals to offend the deities and spirits that were once believed to own and exist within these resources.

A casual examination of folklore, beliefs, and proverbs across Africa reveals a very intricate tapestry unerringly woven around the abundant biodiversity that people interacted with on a daily basis. Even with the current decline in vernacular language use in contemporary African societies, this innate awareness still exists in names. In Kenya, this spreads right across the ethnic spectrum with children named Njogu (*Gikuyu, elephant*), Nyaga (*Gikuyu, ostrich*), Mbiti (*Kamba, hyena*), Munyambu (*Kamba, lion*), Muruthi (*Gikuyu, lion*), Sibuor (*Luo, lion*), Kwach (*Luo, leopard*), Rachier (*Luo, black mamba*), and many others, including place names that were taken from the wild animals found there. Why then, in this day and age, do we find the entire conservation sector devoting an inordinate amount of energy and millions of dollars towards something called awareness? The exogenous (and sometimes racist subtext) in awareness campaigns or conservation education efforts as practiced in Kenya and much of Africa is inescapable.

Behind all this apparently aimless effort and wastage is the overwhelming need for foreign interests to erase our indigenous interpretation of our natural heritage, and indeed of ourselves. That need stems from an insatiable hunger for enduring fame and relevance. Gone are the days when Henry Morton Stanley and his contemporaries would reap fame, fortune, and immortality just by venturing into the dark continent called Africa. Nowadays, Africa is known to be so much more than a land mass: it is a way of thinking; it is almost boundless human resources in terms of numbers and energy; it is huge mineral, plant, and animal resources.

It is these characteristics of our continent that have the power to confer fame and fortune to any outsider who can contrive (or claim) to own a piece of them without even a rudimentary understanding of our history. Like sloths, we have slept as our vision of ourselves, the very core of our identity, has been subverted by interests that grew from the atmosphere of our oppression and have survived the advent of our freedom.

There are few better examples of this than the much-vaunted homecoming of our illustrious daughter, Lupita Nyong'o, the first African actress to win an Academy Award. This is an educated, young Kenyan lady whose elite background, parental support, and hard work have brought her spectacular success on a global stage in her chosen field. As is typical of Kenyans, her ascension to stardom was much celebrated and her homecoming as a star eagerly awaited. When she arrived home in early July 2015, Kenyans were treated to a gushing monologue from one of their own on how important elephants are, how elephant herds are led by a matriarch, and how intelligent these creatures are—all presented to us as reasons why we shouldn't kill them. Her speeches were full of regurgitations, including clichés like "A live elephant is worth a million dollars to the Kenyan economy" and "An elephant is poached every fifteen minutes," and we were inundated with images of her with and around elephants. The fact that neither of these claims can stand up to mathematical examination was lost in the backslapping and clinking of glasses as the buccaneers celebrated the capture of an indigenous face to burnish and cleanse their exotic agenda.

Less knowledgeable observers of this visit were puzzled as to why an indigenous Kenyan, who has lived among us and all our challenges, should suddenly prioritize elephants so stridently. Fans, who had followed her acting career locally in the theater and on various television series, were also puzzled, because nobody could remember her saying anything about wildlife or elephants before she left our shores. Those in the know would notice that she said not a word about human-wildlife conflict, not a word about the symbolism of elephants in local lore and their intrinsic value to us. She talked about the values these animals and their habitats held for the outsiders who somehow took ownership of her much-touted return home.

Any doubts that still existed as to the power and reach of this rapacious company would be thoroughly dispelled on July 26, 2015. The President of the United States, Barack Obama, was at the final engagement of a historic visit to his father's homeland—a town hall style meeting with members of the Kenyan civil society. The company present included human-rights activists, educationists, members of religious organizations, land-rights activists, gender-rights activists, and child-welfare activists. Due to a tight schedule, President Obama graciously chose not to give a speech but to listen to the voices of Kenya's people. Someone helpfully gave him a list of names of people to call upon to highlight issues. The first two names on the list were Tom Lalampaa of the Northern Rangelands Trust and Dr. Paula Kahumbu of Wildlife Direct.

Through Lalampaa, the myth of community driven conservation was fed directly to the whole world in the glare of cameras focused on the holder of the world's most powerful office. It's architect, Ian Craig, nodded sagely next to Tom. Next, the myths of an elephant killed every fifteen minutes and the use of the ivory trade to finance terrorism were administered to President Obama by Dr. Kahumbu, with the assurance of one who has told these tales so many times that they now ring true. Her statement was completed with a typical self-promoting statement that she does what she does because she loves elephants and would like everyone to fall in love with elephants so that we can conserve them. This fallacy was best addressed by Ted Malanda, writing about Lupita Nyongo's homecoming in *The Star* newspaper of July 4, 2015. He wrote, "If you want to save elephants, never say you love them. Revere and fear them. Love blinds one to reality." He may as well have been speaking to Kenya as a nation.

As a country, we have refused to interrogate what emerges from the mouths of the very people who have taken every opportunity to declare their love for our heritage. Neither have we been keen to connect historical and contemporary dots to come to grips with the schemes devised by some (not all) to forever control our resources—even though these dots are as glaring as daylight. In this regard, a country that is so far from economically emancipating itself, a country that is yet to exhaustively determine the nature and extent of its natural wealth, has failed (or refused) to see the connection between the conservation agenda thrust down its throat and the desire of the West to have it maintain its status quo of powerlessness and poverty.

It is far outside the realm of acceptability that remnants of the colonial order, their kith and kin, and newcomers have maintained an unbroken surveillance of vast areas with huge mineral potential under the guise of wildlife conservation. It defies belief that a country with a working government and clandestine outfits can allow close to 10 percent of its territory to be under the control of the Northern Rangelands Trust, an organisation that has very little to show for the billions of shillings it receives from external sources. It is even more disturbing that the NRT has secured total, unquestioning support from a rent-seeking local leadership, some of whom it has named as its directors, and has facilitated the advanced military training of conservation militias who are passed on as game scouts in the conservancies that now owe allegiance to it. Besides other things, this demonstrates a worrisome disconnect between a country seeking to detach itself from a dark past and its inability to shrug itself away from a continuum in which local leadership aided the British colonial administration to rob, kill, maim, and destroy local people and their cultures, as well as their livelihoods.

We must collectively embrace this reality if we are to take ownership of our natural heritage and responsibility for our future. This includes turning away from the fallacies peddled to us about the need to love wildlife and embracing the reality that this precious natural heritage is present in our folklore, culture, names, and our very identity. We must also remember that the communities that still cling to their cultures, despite the fatal influence of modernity, have some of the best preserved resources in the country. Surely, there must be something good to be found in African traditional conservation ethics and practices. We must unearth what can be used and marry it with other approaches to secure wildlife into the undetermined future. We cannot lose the wildlife without losing part of ourselves.

Our reality is constantly changing, and embracing it is about embracing a new way of observation, thought, and interpretation thereof. All is not lost, and there is evidence that our leadership may be picking up a whiff of this reality. As the glossy veneer over the practice of tourism as a basis for conservation begins to wear thin, the major conservation players in northern Kenya are beginning to harp on security as their key intervention in the area and the key benefit that communities are reaping from their conservation activities. Few people stop to think about how violent flare-ups and skirmishes between pastoralist communities continue to occur at the edges of secure conservancies. It is a fact that many of these communities have harboured deep mistrust for conservancies over several generations, but their hostility was mitigated by the geographical distance between themselves and the conservancies that ensured they would seldom meet. Now that conservation initiatives have condemned communities to sharing the limited space on the peripheries of their traditional grazing lands, contact between these foes is increasing, and the results are there for all to see in Kapedo, Baragoi, Suguta Valley, Nginyang', and other flashpoints. After the country was left reeling by the loss of dozens of policemen to so-called bandit attacks, President Uhuru Kenyatta issued the following statement on November 2, 2014:

> Today I visited Chesitet and Kapedo villages which have been hit by recent bandit attacks leading to the death of police officers and civilians, and destruction of property. I ordered Pokot and Turkana residents and their leaders to immediately surrender all illegal guns to the Government. As Government, we will take firm action against those who killed security officers in this area. These criminals must pay for their heinous acts. The Government will not, at any cost, allow criminals to continue taking up arms against the country's security personnel. We will not tolerate anybody threatening the lives of police officers or any other Kenyan. No one has the right to kill another, whatever the reason. As your leader, I will do everything within my Constitutional mandate to ensure the lives of all Kenyans and their property are protected. I cautioned leaders to stop inciting citizens and politicizing natural resources and instead allow investors to extract minerals for the benefit of the country. These resources are supposed to benefit us as Kenyans and not be a source of conflict. We would rather not exploit them in order to maintain peace rather than allow them to divide us. We cannot allow resources such as grazing land, geothermal and oil discoveries to be used as an excuse to maim and kill people. These resources are for the benefit of all Kenyans.

This statement from the highest office in Kenya shows a high degree of awareness, and should give us all a ray of hope as we seek to take responsibility for our natural heritage for the benefit of all mankind. The divisions that lead to violent resource conflicts in Kenya can only be healed through a consultative process to define Kenya's national conservation (or heritage) agenda. This is a process that would set priorities as to what we want to conserve and would encompass cultures (or components thereof), species, ecosystems, buildings, sacred sites, and monuments, among others. This process would define our objectives, which would in turn guide the licensing of conservation research and the allocation of funds thereto. Conservation should never mean a country in stasis, so development players and agencies need to table their agendas during this process in order to find common ground. Resources would then flow into the channels of equitable discourse rather than into the pockets of those who are best at fighting for only a single, narrow end game. In light of the fact that Kenyan societies and ecosystems are dynamic, this proposed dialogue could be held every five years in order to disseminate new findings and review priorities. Kenyan society is very active on various media platforms, and such events would ensure that the dialogue on conservation is a constantly simmering pot that commands the nation's attention. We must remember that there are always beneficiaries of our ignorance and our resultant silence regarding natural resources. In the same vein, we must adopt and nurture a culture of planning as a country. We are constantly bombarded with fallacious arguments by those who have maintained a desire to shape and maintain Africa as a place befitting their own figments of imagination. We are told that our population growth and size are just too high. They justify this with the fact that we do not effectively control development, that besides urban sprawl (that threatens to convert a large section of the country into one huge slum), Kenyans have been spilling over into critically important and ecologically fragile ecosystems that need to be preserved. However, with proper spatial planning, a national and political goodwill and determination, commitment to implement these plans, and a national effort to control greed, we can convert the country into a place that can comfortably support twice or thrice the size of our current population and still leave adequate room for the preservation of species.

What is so attractive about spatial planning is that it is participatory, employs a diversity of professionals, embraces every aspect of society, is forward-looking, and is a tool we can use to anticipate, prepare for, and lessen our vulnerabilities to the emerging negative effects of climate change and other potential catastrophes. The authors believe that besides a lack of local input and effective participation in conservation, spatial planning has been one of the missing elements in wildlife conservation in Kenya. We note that since 2015, some elements within the conservation fraternity (i.e., the usual suspects) have been talking about embracing spatial planning in conservation. But we are concerned that in the absence of widespread public participation and a national conservation dialogue, out of which planning for the future of wildlife will be taken up and facilitated through funding from the exchequer, such piecemeal NGO efforts will end up as yet one more lucrative venture so-called conservationists will use to secure additional donor funding for their opulent lifestyles.

Tourism is undoubtedly an important industry, but we must own the product before trying to sell it to outsiders. As is the case in our homes, visitors should come to see us as we are because of their interest in us, our home, and all that is within. We do not contrive to make and shape our homes in a way that will please visitors. Likewise, on a national level, tourism should not be based on falsification of circumstances, and conservation must not exclude our thoughts, culture, livelihoods, and identities. This kind of tourism defiles a nation and its people and is best captured by this memorable critique from Jeremy Seabrook, a freelance journalist based in the UK:

> Tourism consumes the places on which it alights, predatory, omnivorous and yet protected from any contact with disagreeable realities like poverty, squalor, crime and violence. It sanitizes and cleanses, offering people an experience prepackaged in the great factory of illusion, sensations crafted by an industry which masks real relationships in the world.

If one replaced the words *tourism* with *prostitution* and *places* with *people*, this statement would still have the ring of profound truth about it, but that is another story for another day.

The weight of the arguments we have put forward in this book cannot possibly be overstated, but by that token, they are arguments and conversations Kenya *must* have as a nation. We cannot possibly know how we are going and grow if we do not understand where we came from and where we currently are. The status quo, vis-à-vis wildlife and environmental conservation, has become so entrenched in our society that it has intimidated our best and brightest minds into silent acquiescence or exile. In the course of this work, we both encountered publishers unwilling to handle the manuscript and intimidated scholars reluctant to confront the issues. One of the saddest signs of our times is the stark racial divide in conservation thought, which almost always cut across academic qualifications, professional positions, and old friendships we have nurtured for years. To the few who saw beyond the colour of our skin and interrogated our arguments, you are the precious gems who make this work worth the effort, the reminder of our shared humanity. We thank you.

We will measure our success by the number of people who are pleased by this book, amused by it, and even those who are angered by it, because we will have touched their humanity in some way. It would only be tragic if one read it and remained indifferent.

~ J. Mbaria & M. Ogada.

Nairobi, 2016

REFERENCES:

1. *African Studies* 70, no. 2 (2011) *"Heritage, History and Memory: New Research from East and Southern Africa."*
2. Adamson G. 1968. *Bwana Game; The Life story of George Adamson.*
3. Adamson G. 1987. *My Pride and Joy: An Autobiography.*
4. BBC. June 16, 2003. "Paul van Vlissingen Planned to take over Parks in Zambia, Malawi, Uganda, Kenya and Mozambique."
5. Boudreaux K. 2003. "Community-based Natural Resource Management and Poverty Alleviation in Namibia: A Case Study." Mercatus Center, George Mason University
6. Lutta, S. "Turkana Declares Six Conservancies Illegal Over Permit." *Business Daily.* (January 21, 2016).
7. Capoccia R. E. 2013. "The Impact of Animal Rights on Wildlife Conservation and Management in Kenya." New Brunswick, New Jersey.
8. Carrier N. 2011. "Reviving Yaaku: Identity and Indigeneity in Northern Kenya." *–African Studies* 70, no. 2. Oxford University.
9. Chambers R. 1973. "The Pekerra Irrigation Scheme: A Contrasting Case" *Welt Forum.* Verlag, Munchen.
10. Craig, R., Kamau E. & Malpas, R. 2004. "The Nature and Role of Local Benefits in GEF Program Areas: Pilot Case Study Kenya: Lewa Wildlife Conservancy." Global Environmental Facility Office of Monitoring & Evaluation.
11. Curtis M. 2016. "The New Colonialism: Britain's Scramble for Africa's Energy & Mineral Resources." War on Want.
12. Douglas A. "The Oligarch's Real Game is Killing Animals and Killing People." *EIR.* 21, no. 43 (October 28, 1994).
13. Ghelleh, A. "NGOs in Africa: Assets or Liabilities?" *The Herald* (April 25, 2013).
14. Hallinan C. "Militarizing Africa" *Foreign Policy in Focus* (March 20, 2007).
15. Hemingway E. 2004. *Green Hills of Africa.* Vintage Classics.
16. Hughes, L. 2002. *Moving the Maasai: A Colonial Misadventure.* St Antony's College, Oxford University.

17. Njoroge G. "Current Events on the African Continent." *CNN* (September 11, 2004, 12:30:00 ET).
18. Isiguzo A. I. "African Culture and Symbolism: A Rediscovery of the Seam of a Fragmented Identity."
19. *Kenya Elephant Dilemma* (IWMC Newsletter). Republished in *African Idaba* 1, no .3 (May 2003).
20. Northern Rangelands Trust. 2011. "State of the Conservancies Report."
21. Parker, I. 2004. *What I Tell You Three Times is True: Conservation, Ivory, History and Politics.* Librario Publishing Ltd., UK.
22. Steinhart, E. I. 2006. *Black Poachers, White Hunters: A Social History of Hunting in Colonial Kenya.* Ohio University Press.
23. Gibson, C. C. 1999. *Politicians and Poachers.* Cambridge University Press.
24. GOK. 2015. *Kenya Mining Investment Handbook.*
25. Chapin, M. 2004. *A Challenge to Conservationists.* World Watch Magazine.
26. Rhode, D. L. & Packel A. K. 2009. *Ethics and Non-Profits.* Stanford Social Innovation Review.
27. Ogada, M. O. & Nyingi, D. W. 2013. "The Management of Wildlife and Fisheries Resources in Kenya: Origins, Present Challenges and Future Perspectives." *Developments in Earth Surface Processes* 16. Elsevier.
28. Ogada, M. O. 'Environmental Impact Assessment: Our Enduring Embarrassment."
29. Parker, I. & Bleazard, S.(edits). 2002. *An Impossible Dream: Some of Kenya's Last Colonial Wardens Recall the Game Department in the Closing Years of the British Empire.*
30. Kenyatta, J. 1938. *Facing Mount Kenya.* Secker & Warburg, London.
31. *Business Daily.* (March 24, 2016).
32. Cook, R. 1999. *More dangerous Ground: The Inside Story of Britain's Best Known Investigative Journalist.* Book Guild Publishing, Sussex.
33. Cumming, E. 2015. "Save the Elephants Pioneer Iain Douglas-Hamilton and His Daughter Saba on Their

Special Relationship." *The Guardian* (August 30, 2015).
34. Durrell, G. 1950. *The Bafut Beagles*. Penguin Books.
35. Durrell, G. 1960. *A Zoo in My Luggage*. Penguin Books.
36. Turner, V. 1971. *Colonialism in Africa 1870-1960: Volume III Profiles of Change: African Society and Colonial Rule*. Cambridge University Press.
37. Leakey, L. S. B. 1977. *The Southern Kikuyu Before 1903*. Academic Press.
38. Leakey, R. M. 2001. *Wildlife Wars: My Fight to Save Africa's Natural Treasures*. St. Martin's Press.
39. Elkins, C. 2005. *Imperial Reckoning: The Untold Story of Britain's Gulag in Kenya*. Henry Holt.
40. Government of Kenya 2012. Sessional Paper No. 14 of 2012 on Reforming Education & Training Sectors in Kenya.
41. Kariuki, J. "Rancher's 18-Year Woes as Squatters Ignore Eviction Orders." *Daily Nation* (July 15, 2014).
42. Kinlock, B. 2004. *The Shamba Raiders: Memories of a Game Warden*.
43. Koinante, J. 2011. "Mukogodo, Mau and Kaya Forests in Kenya." United Nations Department of Economic & Social Affairs, Division for Social Policy and Development.
44. Loefler, I. "A New Game Plan for Wildlife Conservation." *African Indaba* 1, no. 3 (2003).
45. Malakoff, D. "Kenya Parks Chief Ousted—Again." *Science* 281, no. 5385 (September 21, 1998).
46. Manji, F. 2002. "The Missionary Position: NGOs and Development in Africa." *Pambazuka News*.
47. Mbaria, J. 2004. "Maasai Reject IUCN Project in Loita Forest." *The EastAfrican*. Nation Media Group Ltd.
48. Mbaria, J. 2007.- "Our Land is Dying" *Daily Nation* Nation Media Group Ltd.
49. Mbaria, J. "At the Root of the Poaching Menace is a Veritable Clash of Value Systems." *Daily Nation* (March 24, 2014).
50. Mbaria, J. 2006. "Assault of the Biopirates." *The EastAfrican*.
51. Mbaria, J. "Conservation NGO Kicked Out of Samburu Over 'Vested Interests.'" *The EastAfrican* (May 14, 2007).

52. Mbaria, J. 2010. "Exploring 'Green Travel' on Earth Day, from a Kenyan's Perspective" *Investigate West Online Journal.*

53. Mbaria, J. "How the West Blatantly Finances and Directs Kenya's Law Making Processes." *Sunday Nation* (July 2007).

54. Mbaria, J. "KWS Seeks Millions from Procter & Gamble." *The EastAfrican* (August 23, 2004).

55. Mbaria, J. "African Violet Blues: Why Hasn't This Million-Dollar Flower from the Taita Hills Made the Local People Rich?" *The Eastafrican* (May 31–June 6, 2004).

56. McGown, J. 2006. "Out of Africa: Mysteries of Access and Benefit Sharing." Edmonds Institute & African Centre for Biosafety.

57. Munyi, P. "Commercialisation of Alkaliphilic Bacteria Originating from Kenya." Southern Environmental and Agricultural Policy Research Institute, International Centre of Insect Physiology and Ecology, Kenya.

58. National Environment Management Authority. 2007. "Field Visit Report: Samburu and Buffalo Springs National Reserves" (April 18-19, 2007).

59. Norton-Griffiths, M. "The Economics of Land Use in the Mara Area."

60. Norton-Griffiths, M. "Reflections from a Mature Student."

61. Norton-Griffiths, M. "The Opportunity Cost of Biodiversity Conservation in Kenya." Centre for Social and Economic Research on the Global Environment, University College London.

62. Norton-Griffith, M. "Protected Areas Management by Private Landowners: The Case for Private Sector Investments in Conservation: An African Perspective."

63. Norton-Griffiths, M. "Wildlife Conservation on Kenya's Rangelands: An Economic Perspective."

64. Ogot, B. A. 2003. *My Footprints on the Sands of Time: An Autobiography.* Trafford Publishing.

65. Pels, P. 1997. "The Anthropology of Colonialism: Culture, History, and the Emergence of Western Governmentality." Research Centre Religion and Society, University of Amsterdam.

66. Ratemo, J. 2007. "Dr. Imre Loefler is No Longer on Call." *The Standard* (March 16, 2007).

67. Rugene, N. & Kenya News Agency. 1998. "Moi Criticizes Western." *Daily Nation.*
68. Odengo, R. "Poaching of Mount Kenya Bush Viper." Kenya Broadcasting Corporation (February 23, 2007).
69. Kahindi, O. "Cultural Perception of the Elephant by the Samburu of Northern Kenya." MSc. thesis, University of Strathclyde.
70. Silver Bullet PR. "Sir Richard Branson Pledges Airline Support for the David Sheldrick Wildlife Trust."
71. Smith, L. "Big game Trophy Hunters 'Help to Save Rare Species.'"
72. Stiles, D. "The End of Bwana Game: An Appreciation of the Life and Work of George Adamson."
73. Travers, W. 2016. "George Adamson: We all need inspiration in our lives." http://www.bornfree.org.uk/blog/2016/george-adamson/.
74. Thuku, K. 2004. "The Silent Relevance of African Trans-Family Ethnographies: Realities and Reflections on the African Family." *The Family in the New Millennium: The Place of Family in Human Society.* Greenwood Publishing Group.
75. Waithaka, J. ."Historical Factors that Shaped Wildlife Conservation in Kenya." *The George Wright Forum* 29, no. 1 (2012).
76. Waithaka, J. "Kenya Wildlife Service in the 21st Century: Protecting Globally Significant Areas and Resources." *The George Wright Forum* 29, no. 1 (2012).
77. Wikileaks. 2006."Kenya Reply on Sharing of Genetic Resources ." https://www.wikileaks.org/plusd/cables/06NAIROBI117 4_a.html.

ABOUT THE AUTHORS

John Mbaria is a trained spatial planner and an award-winning Kenyan journalist who has investigated and written on wildlife conservation since August 2000. Mbaria started off as a physical planner before detouring to journalism. He has written for several national newspapers in Kenya—the *Daily Nation* and *The* EastAfrican—and was an occasional contributor for the *Greenpeace Magazine* of Germany, as well as a visiting writer with *InvestigateWest*, a US-based online investigative journal.
    gatumbaria@gmail.com

Dr. Mordecai Ogada is a carnivore ecologist who has been involved in conservation work for the last sixteen years in Kenya and other parts of Africa, mainly in human-wildlife conflict mitigation and carnivore conservation. His biological work includes studies on lions, hyenas, cheetah, African wild dogs, and otters. Dr. Ogada's professional work has included research and teaching conservation leadership at Colorado State University. Much of his energy has been devoted to the area of community-based conservation, wildlife policy, and wetlands ecology. From 2009 to 2011 Dr. Ogada developed cheetah conservation strategies for Ethiopia, South Sudan, and Uganda as the regional coordinator for the WCS cheetah conservation program. He was the Executive Director of the Laikipia Wildlife Forum from 2011 to 2014, where his work focused on the perceptions of conservation and how these influence communities and practitioners in the field of natural resource management. In 2015, Dr. Ogada coordinated a partnership project between the African Conservation Centre and McGill University that seeks to strengthen conservation linkages between institutions and habitats in Kenya and northern Tanzania. He is also a co-author of a chapter on the management of wildlife and fisheries in Kenya in the book *Developments in Earth Surface Processes* (Vol 16) published by Elsevier, Netherlands, as well as several articles on conservation. Mordecai lives in Nanyuki, Kenya, where he works as a consultant on wildlife and natural resource conservation.
    mordecai@ogada.co.ke

Made in the USA
San Bernardino, CA
12 August 2017